THE DETROIT PUBLIC LIBRARY

An American Classic

BARBARA MADGY COHN AND PATRICE RAFAIL MERRITT

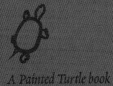

A Painted Turtle book

ISBN 978-0-8143-4232-9 (cloth)
ISBN 978-0-8143-4233-6 (ebook)
Library of Congress Cataloging Number: 2016952138

∞

Painted Turtle is an imprint of Wayne State University Press

Wayne State University Press
Leonard N. Simons Building
4809 Woodward Avenue
Detroit, Michigan 48201-1309

Visit us online at wsupress.wayne.edu

To Andrew Carnegie, whose vision and benevolence provided the world with infinite access to knowledge through such wonderful edifices as the Detroit Public Library

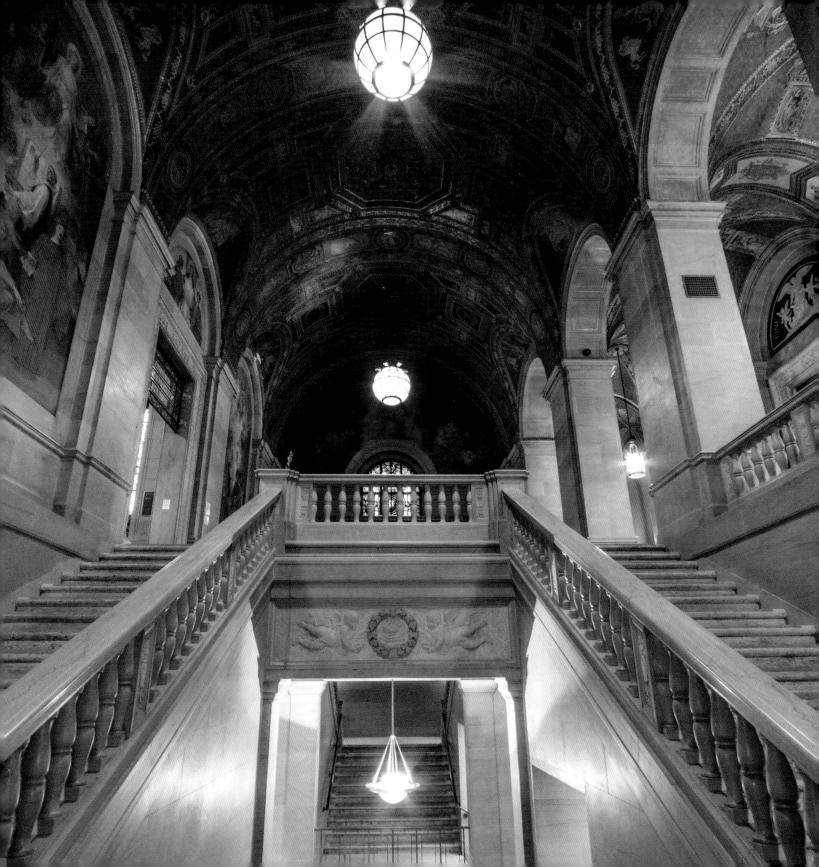

Public buildings best serve the public by being beautiful.

CASS GILBERT

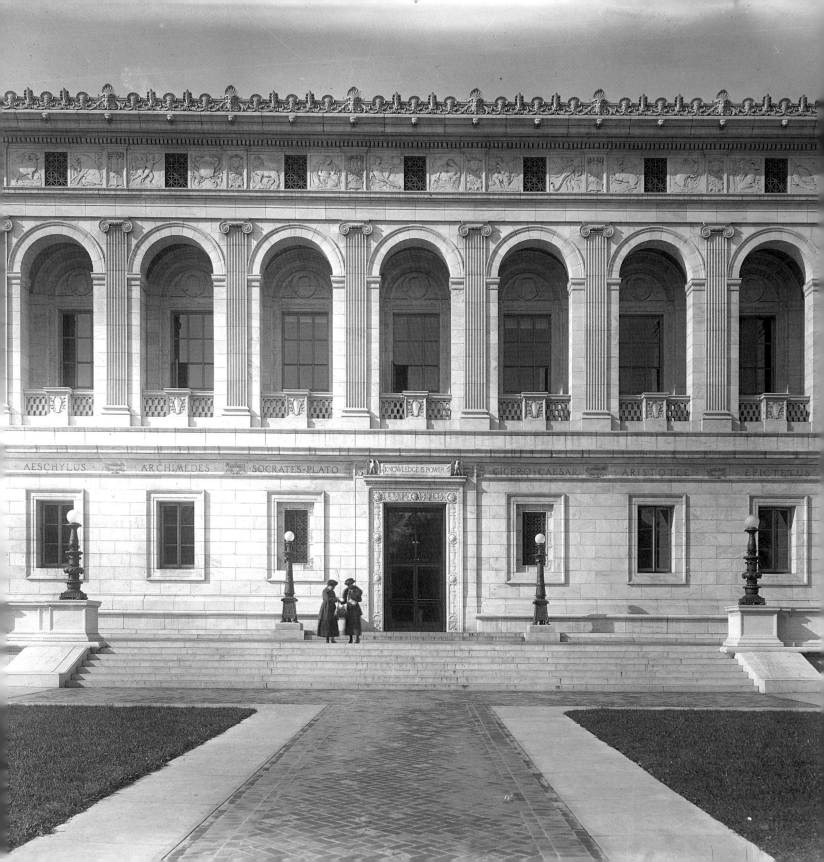

CONTENTS

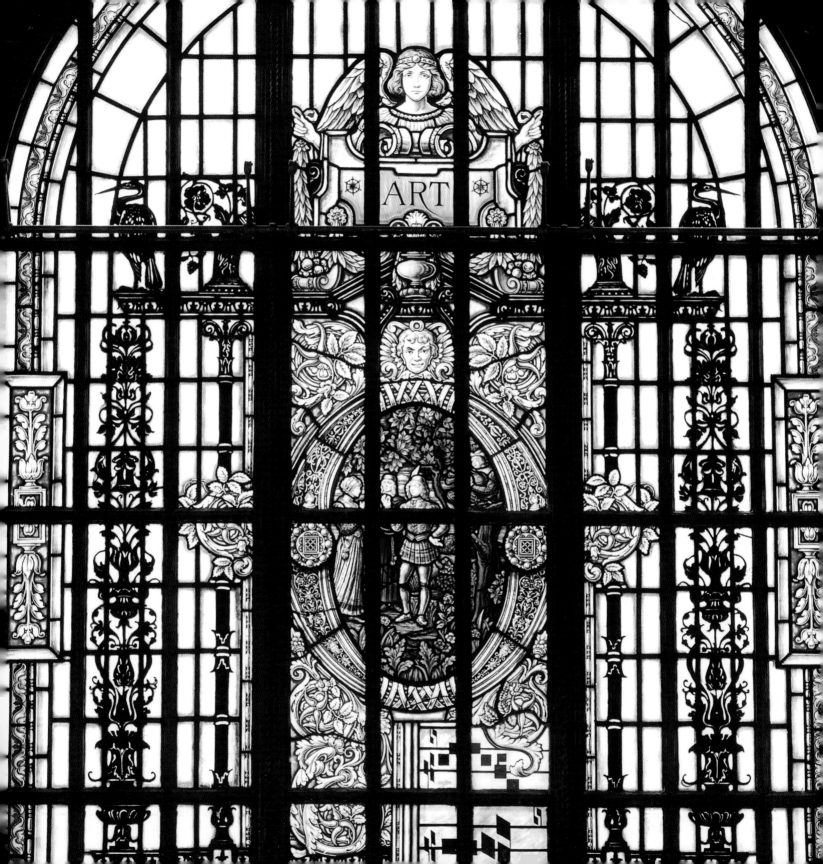

PREFACE

In preparing this book, we had two fundamental goals. The first was to showcase the design of the Main Library using pictures of the past as well as images of the library today as seen through the eyes of Detroit's modern photographers. The second was to share with the world the beauty and elegance of a grand building in a great city that even through difficult times has sustained one of the most magnificent neo-classical buildings in the country. We had an intense desire to ensure that this overlooked treasure was revived and shared.

In 2013, we decided to create a docent-led art and architecture tour of the Main Library for the community to share and enjoy. This was the beginning of our journey. For over ten months, we researched the history of the building of the Main Library, interviewed individuals familiar with its legacy, searched archives, met with staff, and deeply studied the content of the library's special collections. Our journey introduced us to artistic treasures; educated us on the tireless efforts of city fathers who had a vision of grandeur for a growing city; and allowed us to welcome a generation of Detroiters *back* to their Detroit Public Library and invite them to experience the glory of a beautiful building embraced and respected by all who had entered its glorious halls. We organized "test groups" for an initial walking tour and violà! On Saturday, December 7, 2013, the *Discover the Wonders of the Detroit Public Library: An Art and Architectural Tour* was launched.

The response to the tour program far exceeded our expectations. What began as a once-a-month free public tour has grown into a program of private tours for a wide array of regional and national organizations and visitors. However, we remain true to our original mission and continue to offer docent-led tours to the public on a monthly basis.

This book is a direct outcome of the successful tour program. At the conclusion of each tour, docents were repeatedly asked, "Do you have a book for sale?" The response was simply, "Not yet." And thus our second journey began. The photography within this volume captures not only the elegance of the building but also the original vision of Cass Gilbert and the many artisans, local, national, and international, who made his vision a reality. Additionally, we offer this book to honor and recognize the many civic-minded individuals who, throughout the library's history, continued to add gifts of art to the community and its beautiful library building. *The Detroit Public Library: An American Classic* is a tribute to the enduring symbol of the public library, the most democratic of institutions in America.

Barbara Madgy Cohn and Patrice Rafail Merritt
Detroit, Michigan

Photograph courtesy of Kenneth Gabriel.

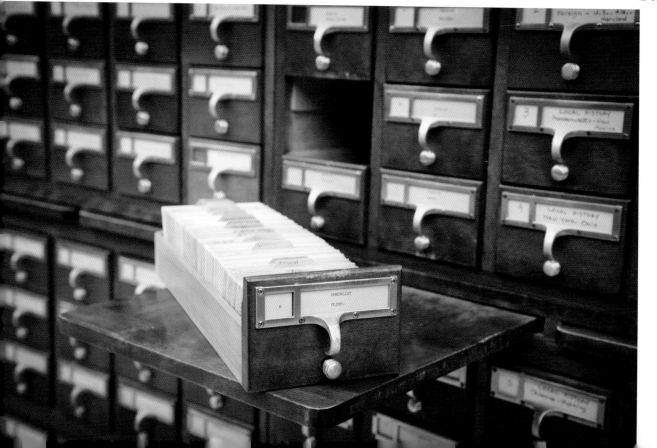

THE DETROIT PUBLIC LIBRARY

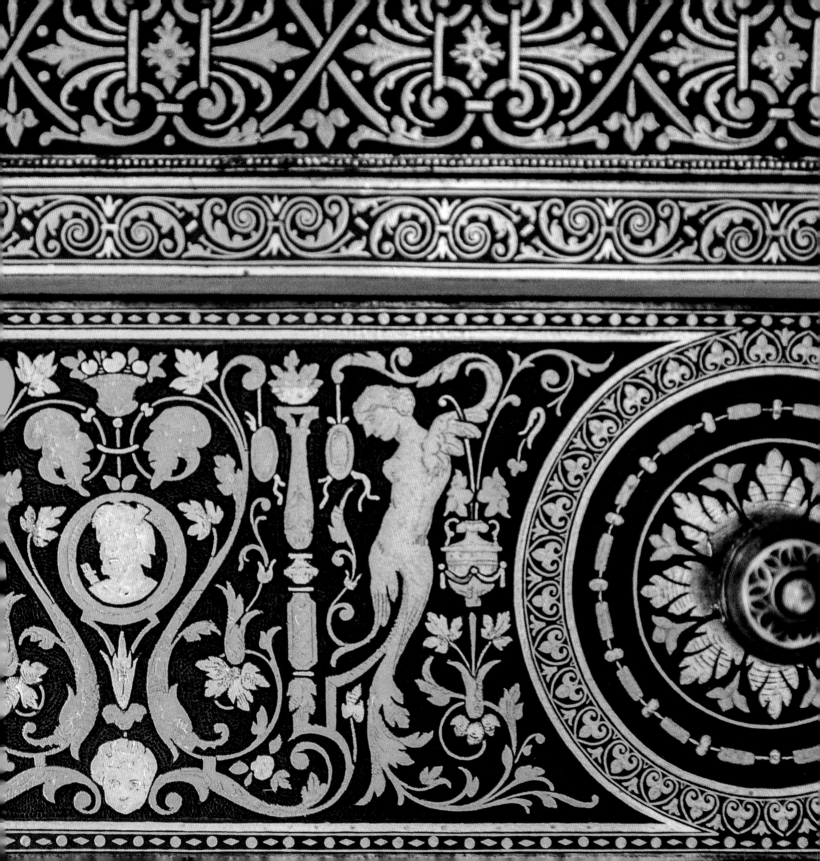

Timeline

1808　First suggestion of record for a public library in Detroit presented to the governor and judges on October 18, 1808, by Father Gabriel Richard. He stated, "It would be very necessary to have in Detroit a Public Building . . . framing a beginning of a public Library."

1835　First constitution of Michigan passed, containing the following clause: "The legislature shall provide for libraries." Michigan was the first state to make this constitutional provision.

1864　Henry Chaney, one of the library commissioners, sent to eastern cities to buy books. He spent $7,000 to purchase 5,000 books.

1865　During the last months of the Civil War, the first library opened in Detroit in a shared, one-room space in the former State Capital Building on Capital Square, located at State and Griswold streets.

1866　Personal library of Lewis Cass (governor of Michigan Territory, 1813–31, U.S. senator representing Michigan, 1849–57) donated to the Detroit Public Library.

1867　German books purchased; beginning of foreign-language collection.

1877　First new library opened, in its own building, at the site of the downtown library at Farmer and Griswold streets.

1880　First Board of Library Commissioners appointed by the Board of Education.

1886　Library implemented Dewey Decimal System.

Telephone installed in library.

1887　Library lighted by electricity.

1891　Polish books added to foreign collection.

1895　Medical library established; transferred to Wayne County Medical School in 1910.

1896　Books in braille available.

1898　Circulation for year exceeded 1,000,000 mark.

1900　First branch opened in Central High School on Cass and Warren avenues.

1901　Special meeting of Library Commission called to consider need for new Main Library building.

Andrew Carnegie offered $750,000 ($375,000 for Main Library building and $375,000 for branch libraries). City asked to submit ballot question regarding issuing $500,000 of library bonds for purpose of complying with Carnegie's offer.

1902 Saturday afternoon story hour for children began.

1903 Ford Motor Company founded.

1907 Voters rejected Carnegie's gift offer but approved $750,000 library bond issue.

1908 General Motors Company founded.

1910 Carnegie offer accepted by Common Council.

1911 Options sought for new Main Library site in Woodward-Kirby-Cass-Putnam block.

1912 First parcel of property for new Main Library site purchased.

Adam Strohm appointed library director (1912–41).

1913 Land purchased on Woodward Avenue site for $416,000.

Architectural contract for new library awarded to Cass Gilbert.

1914 Clarence Monroe Burton donated his private library and established the Burton Historical Collection.

1915 Steel structure completed.

1917 Cornerstone laid for new Main Library.

1921 The 180,000-square-foot library building opened to the public in March 1921 and formally dedicated in June. The building cost was $2,775,000, which included the Carnegie contribution of $375,000. It took six years to complete.

Clarence Monroe Burton established endowment for support of Burton Historical Collection.

1934 Cass Gilbert died (1859–1934).

1940 War Information Center opened at Main Library.

1942 Friends of the Detroit Public Library established.

1943 E. Azalia Hackley Memorial Collection established from a gift of the Detroit Musicians Association.

1944 Cass Gilbert Jr. and Francis Keally named architects for Main Library addition. Plans approved for extending wings to the north and south.

1944 Automotive History Collection established.

1954 American Motors Corporation (AMC) established.

1955 Delivery Room renamed Adam Strohm Hall.

1956 Common Council appropriated $2,500,000 to begin construction of two new wings to the Main Library.

1957 Common Council authorized first issue of library bonds to finance Main Library addition. Construction for addition began.

1960   Cornerstone-laying ceremony for new wing.

1963   Main Library addition dedicated. The building cost $11,700,000, took five years to complete, and added 240,000 square feet.

1966   Ernie Harwell began donating personal sports memorabilia.

1970   Clara Jones appointed first female African American director (1970–78).

1981   Redford Branch opened, the last branch constructed.

1995   Computers installed in the Main Library.

2004   Lulu and Ernie Harwell Room dedicated.

2013   *Discover the Wonders of the Detroit Public Library: An Art and Architectural Tour* created.

2014   Digital Asset Management System implemented, providing access to over 65,000 images.

2015   Detroit Public Library celebrated 150th anniversary (1865–2015).

2017   The Detroit Public Library Friends Foundation 75th Anniversary (1942–2017).

       100th anniversary of the laying of the cornerstone for the Main Library on Woodward Avenue.

2021   100th anniversary of the opening of the Main Library building.

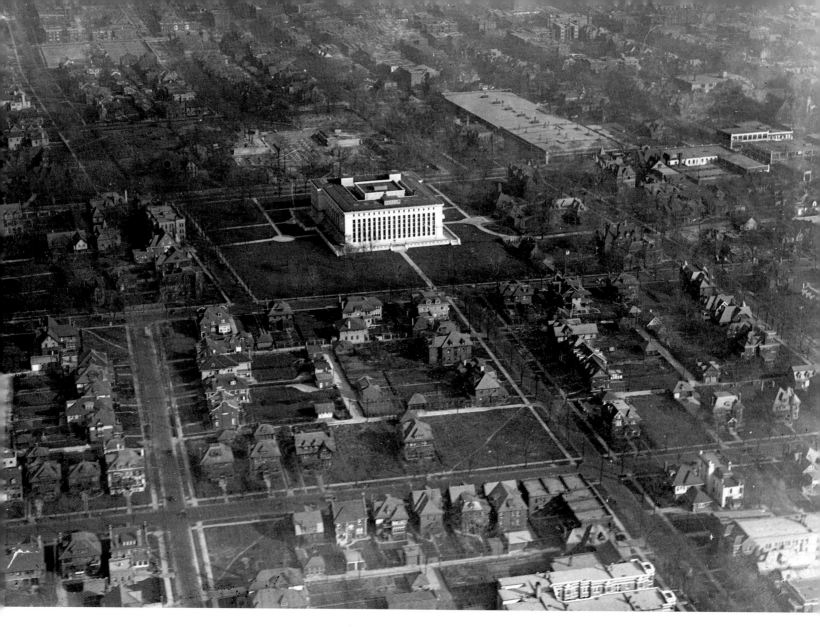

Aerial view of the Detroit Public Library upon completion in 1921. Note that the Detroit Institute of Art was not yet completed and the campus of Wayne State University was primarily a residential community. *Photograph courtesy of the Walter P. Reuther Library, Archives of Labor and Urban Affairs, Wayne State University.*

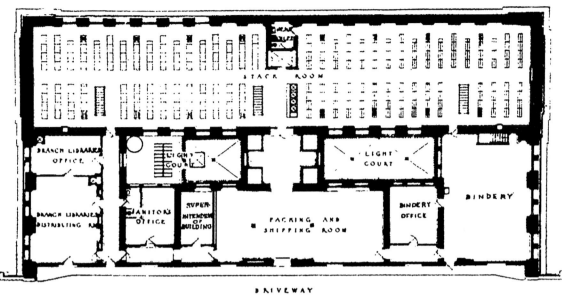

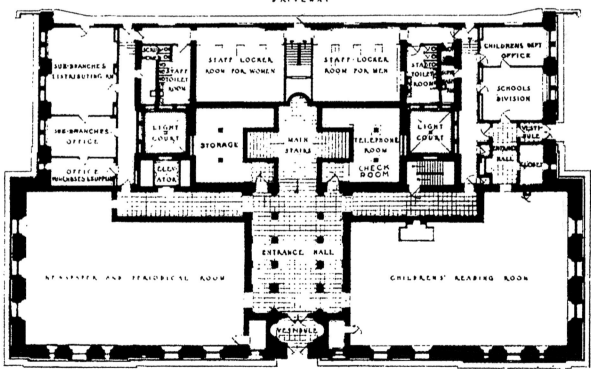

FIRST FLOOR

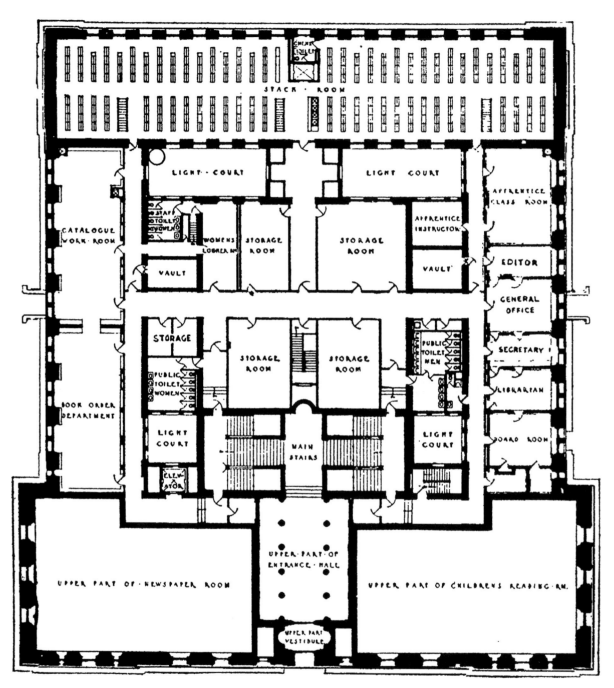

STACK · ROOM

LIGHT · COURT

LIGHT COURT

APPRENTICE
CLASS ROOM

CATALOGUE
WORK ROOM

STAFF
TOILET
WOMEN

WOMENS
LOCKER RM

STORAGE
ROOM

STORAGE
ROOM

APPRENTICE
INSTRUCTOR

EDITOR

VAULT

VAULT

GENERAL
OFFICE

SECRETARY

STORAGE

STORAGE
ROOM

STORAGE
ROOM

PUBLIC
TOILET
MEN

LIBRARIAN

PUBLIC
TOILET
WOMEN

BOOK ORDER
DEPARTMENT

LIGHT
COURT

MAIN
STAIRS

LIGHT
COURT

BOARD ROOM

ELEV-
ATOR

UPPER · PART · OF · NEWSPAPER · ROOM

UPPER · PART · OF
ENTRANCE · HALL

UPPER · PART · OF · CHILDRENS · READING · RM.

UPPER · PART
VESTIBULE

Mezzanine Level

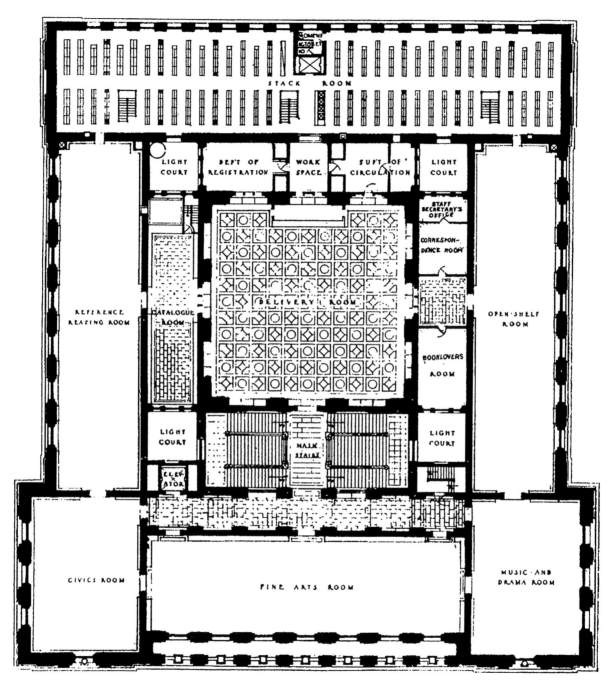

WOMEN'S TOILET

STACK ROOM

LIGHT COURT

DEPT OF REGISTRATION

WORK SPACE

SUP'T OF CIRCULATION

LIGHT COURT

STAFF SECRETARY'S OFFICE

CORRESPONDENCE ROOM

REFERENCE READING ROOM

CATALOGUE ROOM

DELIVERY ROOM

BOOKLOVERS ROOM

OPEN SHELF ROOM

LIGHT COURT

MAIN STAIRS

LIGHT COURT

ELEVATOR

CIVICS ROOM

FINE ARTS ROOM

MUSIC AND DRAMA ROOM

SECOND FLOOR

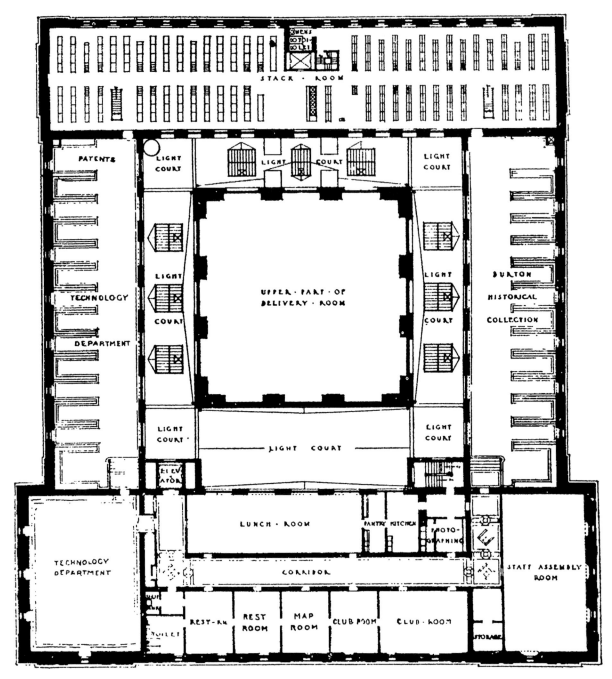

THIRD FLOOR

Building a Library

The Constitution

Michigan was the first state to include a provision for public libraries in its constitution. The first Michigan Constitution (1835) recognized libraries as an integral part of the state's educational system. Article 10, Section 4 states, "As soon as the circumstances of the state will permit, the legislature shall provide for the establishment of Libraries, one at least in each township; and the money shall be paid by persons as an equivalent for exemption from military duty, and the clear proceeds of all fines assessed in the several counties for any breach of the penal laws, shall be exclusively applied for the support of said libraries."

The people of Michigan continued their support of public libraries in the constitutions of 1908 and 1963.

The Philanthropist: Andrew Carnegie (1835–1919)

Born in Dunfermline, Scotland, in 1835, philanthropist and industrialist Andrew Carnegie came to America with his parents in 1848. Settling in Allegheny, Pennsylvania, Carnegie rose from humble beginnings to become a self-made and successful business leader in the late nineteenth century. He created the Carnegie Steel Company, and by 1889 it was the largest steel-producing company in the world. In 1901, Carnegie sold his company to US Steel and began his philanthropic career.

A library outranks any other thing a community can do to benefit its people. It is a never failing spring in the desert.

Andrew Carnegie

A tablet honoring Andrew Carnegie in gratitude for his generosity is located on the north wall of the Entrance Hall. *Photograph courtesy of Martin Vecchio.*

THIS INSCRIPTION
COMMEMORATES THE COMPLETION
OF THE
DETROIT PUBLIC LIBRARY BUILDING
ERECTED BY THE CITY OF DETROIT
FOR THE FREE USE OF ALL HER PEOPLE
1921
—
IN MEMORY OF
ANDREW CARNEGIE
WHOSE GENEROUS AND TIMELY AID
HASTENED THE COMPLETION
OF THIS BUILDING
AND ENLARGED THE SCOPE AND
FUNCTION OF THE LIBRARY

In 1905, Andrew Carnegie created the Carnegie Foundation to promote the advancement and diffusion of knowledge and understanding. His goal was to make free reading materials available in communities throughout the world. Between 1886 and 1919, Carnegie funded some 3,000 libraries located throughout the world. He spent over $55 million on public libraries and is often referred to as the Patron Saint of Libraries.

In the United States there were 1,679 Carnegie libraries, 61 in Michigan alone. In 1901, Carnegie offered $750,000 to the Detroit Public Library Commission, $375,000 of which was to be used for the proposed new Main Library building, and the remaining money was to be applied toward building library branches. Using Carnegie funding, eight library branches were built throughout Detroit neighborhoods: Bowen, Butzel, Conely, Duffield, Ginsburg, Lothrop, Osius, and Utley. The offer was formally accepted in 1910, and the library and City Planning Commission began the planning process.

Carnegie's gift had very specific conditions attached: his money could not be used to purchase sites. His method was to build and equip, but only on the condition that local authorities provided the land and a budget for operation and maintenance. The city was required to supply these, and the library was to be maintained at public expense. There was no perpetual endowment associated with the gift.

THE VISIONARY: CASS GILBERT (1859–1934)

Cass Gilbert was born in Zanesville, Ohio, on November 24, 1859. After his father passed away, the family moved to St. Paul, Minnesota, where he was trained as a surveyor. In 1878 he studied architecture at the Massachusetts Institute of Technology and then traveled to Europe to further his interests in classical antiquity, painting, sculpture, and the great masterpieces. Upon his return to the United States in 1882, he was employed by the architectural firm McKim, Mead, and White of New York before establishing his own practice in St. Paul. As he found success in his practice, Gilbert utilized his architectural commissions to embark upon a tour of Europe to again broaden and complete his education. In 1879, he traveled to England, France, and Italy, observing the classic architectural styles and sites that would influence him for the remainder of his life. In 1887 he married Julia T. Finch. Their marriage produced four children: three daughters, Emily, Elizabeth, and Julia, and one son, Cass Gilbert Jr.

Gilbert was the architect of the Detroit Public Library. He was selected from a two-stage competition of twenty Detroit and national architects to create a stately building on a site that was located in an area slated to become Detroit's Cultural Center for Arts and Letters. Once awarded the contract, Gilbert set off to Italy to seek inspiration, design ideas, and motifs of architecture scattered throughout Florence, Rome, Venice, and Siena. The influences of that expedition are reflected throughout the Detroit Public Library.

Gilbert believed that a library was not only a repository for books but a symbol of the cultural life of the community. Built to reflect an environment of refinement, the exterior of this magnificent edifice is in the Early Italian Renaissance style. The building features glistening white Vermont marble, an ornate cornice executed in terra cotta, balustrade terraces, noble arches, Ionic pilasters, and a second-floor loggia with a colorful mosaic-tiled ceiling. The structure is four floors although the facade creates an illusion of three floors, concealing a mezzanine level. Gilbert's vision was to create a grand library reflecting classical traditions of the golden era of architecture and beauty to inspire people to learn.

Throughout both the exterior and interior are details of ancient Greek and Roman mythology, signs of the zodiac, classic symbolism and ornamentation, architectural elements, and iconography. This building is Cass Gilbert's vision of a combination of form, grace, proportion, history, and beauty.

Taking nearly six years to complete, the building is located on land bordered by Woodward Avenue to the east, Putnam Street to the south, Cass Avenue to the west, and Kirby Street to the north. The design is square, rising 60 feet in height. Over the perfectly centered entrance doors is the inscription "Knowledge Is Power."

Gilbert was a conservative who strongly believed architecture should serve a social order and reflect historic traditions. He was a prominent American architect, and his numerous works included museums, libraries, federal and state buildings, and commercial and private designs. Some of his remarkable works include the sixty-story Woolworth Skyscraper Building in New York City (1910–13), the United States Treasury Annex (1918–19), the Supreme Court building in Washington, D.C. (1935), the Minnesota state capital (1895–1905), the St. Louis Art Museum (1904), the St. Louis Public Library (1908–10), the Allen Memorial Art Museum at Oberlin College in Cincinnati, Ohio (1917), and the James Scott Memorial Fountain on Belle Isle in Detroit (1925). He also planned the campuses of Universities of Minnesota (Minneapolis) and Texas (Austin). In 1906 he was elected into the National Academy of Design as an associate member and a full academician in 1908. He was elected president of the American Institute of Architects and appointed to the National Commission of Fine Arts. He died in Brockenhurst, England.

Paragraph from a letter from Cass Gilbert to Detroit Public Library director Adam Strohm, March 28, 1917.

> Detroit needs a new library very much. It should have it as soon as possible. It should be well built of good materials. It should have that beauty and distinction which will respond to the just pride of the City. It is one of the structures which will most be noted by citizens and strangers alike as the evidence of the civic spirit, the progressive character and the intelligence of the community.

The Designer: Frederick J. Wiley
(1856–1932)

Born in Detroit, Frederick J. Wiley was the son of noted Detroiter Jefferson Wiley, the owner of the hardware firm Prentiss & Wiley. His brother, George Wiley, was president of the Wayne County Home and Savings Bank. Frederick J. Wiley attended the Patterson School and later studied law at Harvard, graduating in 1877. Wiley practiced law in Detroit in the office of John H. Bissell until 1885, when he relocated to New York. Wiley gave up law and dedicated his life to the study of decoration and established a design firm with W. Francklyn Paris later known as Paris & Wiley, Architectural Artists. In 1919, he returned to Detroit at the request of architect Cass Gilbert to work on the murals to be installed in the new library. Upon receiving the commission, Wiley spent several months in Italy to study the masterpieces of classical design, which would later be incorporated in his work at the Detroit Public Library. The library was not Wiley's first collaboration with Cass Gilbert. In 1917, Gilbert designed the Allen Memorial Art Museum at Oberlin College in Cincinnati, Ohio, with Wiley providing the interior design. Wiley died in New York at the age of seventy-six.

WORKS:
Loggia ceiling
Loggia floor
Pictorial map of Michigan, 1923
Fourteen painted windows
Vestibule and third-floor ceilings

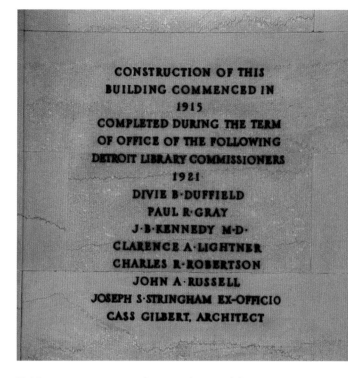

Tablet commemorating the completion of the Detroit Public Library located on the south wall of the Entrance Hall. *Photograph courtesy of Timothy Griffin.*

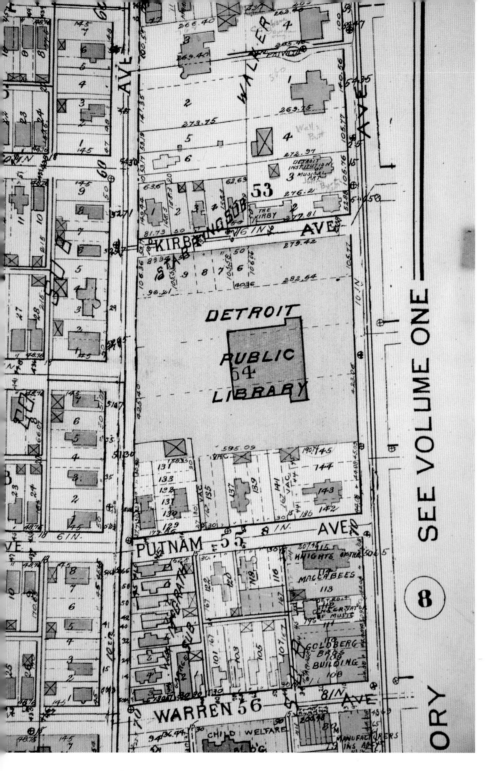

A 1923 Sanborn Map of Detroit details the location of the Main Library between Kirby and Putnam streets. Note that some land parcels on the library site had not been purchased by the Library Commission. The Sanborn Fire Insurance Map Company was established in 1867. Maps were originally created for assessing fire insurance liability in urbanized areas throughout United States. The maps are large, lithographed street plans at a scale of 50 feet to one inch on sheets of paper measuring 21 by 25 inches. Published in volumes, the maps were bound and updated until a subsequent volume was produced. In between the publication of volumes, drawings of new or altered buildings or lots were created and pasted (known as "slips") on top of the old maps to reduce expense and preserve accuracy.

The map volumes contain an enormous amount of information. The maps include outlines of each building, the location of windows and doors, street names, street and sidewalk widths, property boundaries, fire walls, natural features (waterways), railroad corridors, building use, house and block number; and the composition of building materials, locations of fire hydrants, locations of water and gas mains, and names of public buildings, churches, and businesses.

Photograph courtesy of Kenneth Gabriel.

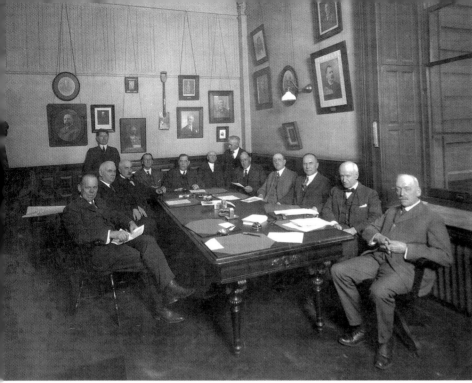

TOP: Cass Gilbert surrounded by the artists and leaders responsible for the development of his vision. From lower left clockwise: Paul Gray, J. A. Russell, Gari Melcher, Adam Strohm (standing), J. S. Stringham, J. B. Kennedy, Edwin H. Blashfield, Charles R. Robertson (standing), Divie B. Duffield, Cass Gilbert, John J. Rockart, Frederick J. Wiley, and Clarence Monroe Burton. *Photograph courtesy of the Burton Historical Collection, Detroit Public Library.*

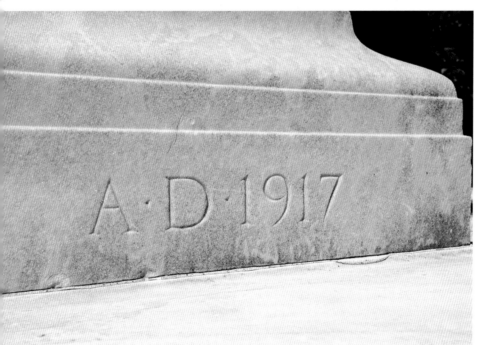

BOTTOM: The cornerstone today, located at the northeast corner of the Main Library at Kirby Street and Woodward Avenue. *Photograph courtesy of John Campbell.*

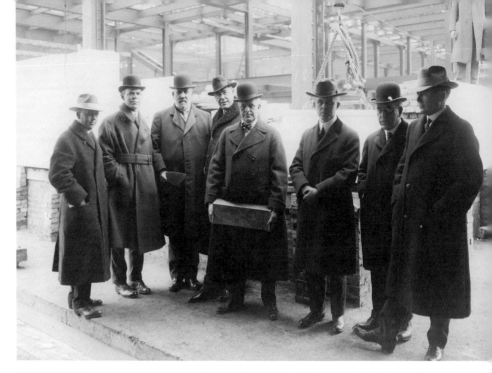

TOP: The laying of the cornerstone, November 1, 1917. Pictured left to right: Edward Piggins, Paul Gray, Ralph Phelps, J. B. Kennedy, Mayor Oscar Marx, Samuel Mumford, Bernard Ginsburg, and library director Adam Strohm. *Photo courtesy of the Burton Historical Collection, Detroit Public Library.*

BOTTOM: Clarence M. Burton attends the ground-breaking ceremony for the new Detroit Public Library, January 12, 1915. *Photograph courtesy of the Burton Historical Collection, Detroit Public Library.*

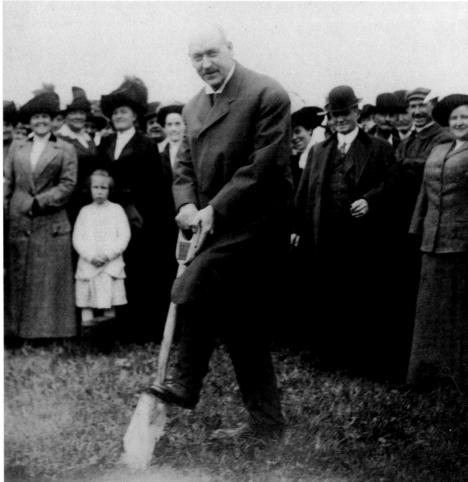

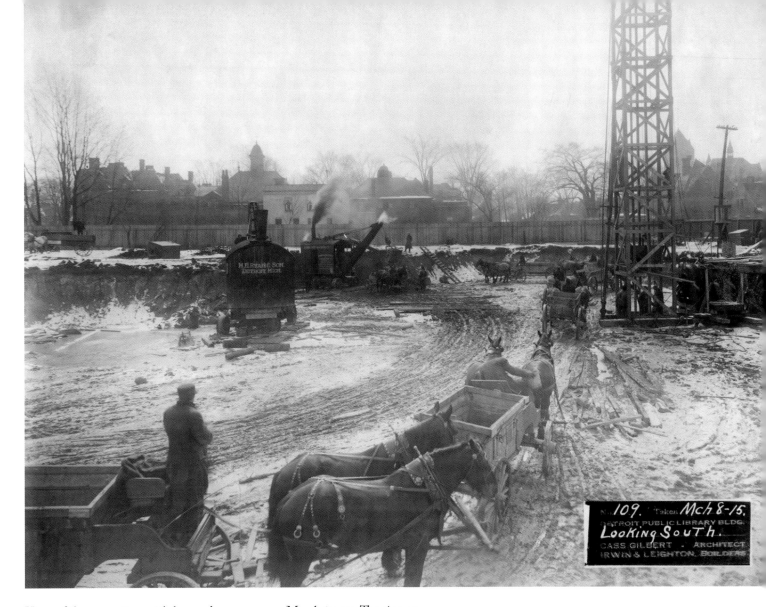

View of the excavation with horse-drawn wagons, March 8, 1915. The sign on the steam shovel reads "M. E. Ryan & Son, Detroit, Mich." Photograph by Charles Ruel Messenger. *Photograph courtesy of the Burton Historical Collection, Detroit Public Library.*

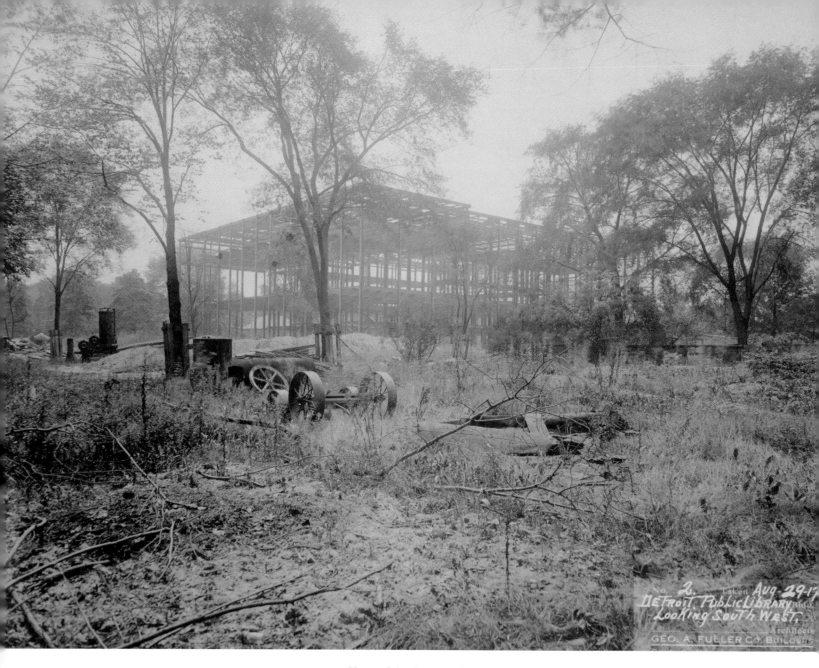

View of the framework arising from an overgrown field with wheels and other debris, August 29, 1917. Photograph by Charles Ruel Messenger.
Photograph courtesy of the Burton Historical Collection, Detroit Public Library.

View of the framework of the Detroit Public Library, 1916. The structure is surrounded by a wooden fence with a sign reading "Vote yes in favor of the new Main Library, November 7th." The bond issue was approved by voters on November 9, 1916. *Photograph courtesy of the Burton Historical Collection, Detroit Public Library.*

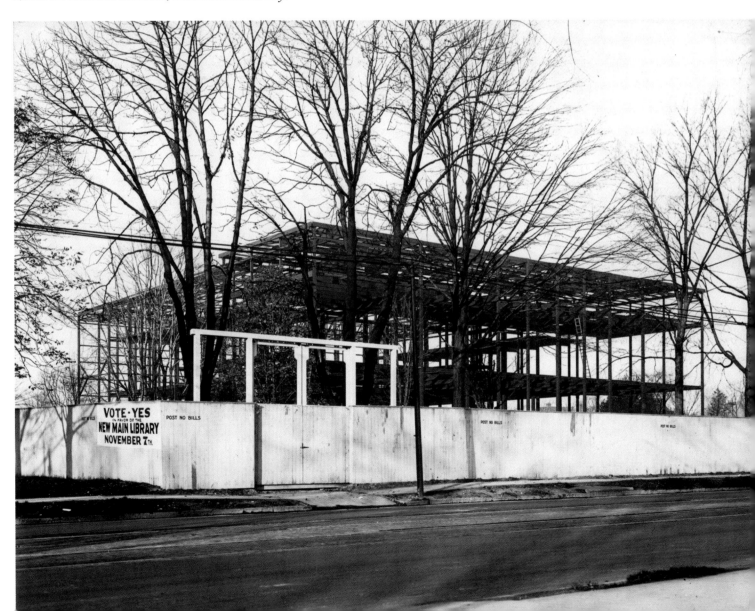

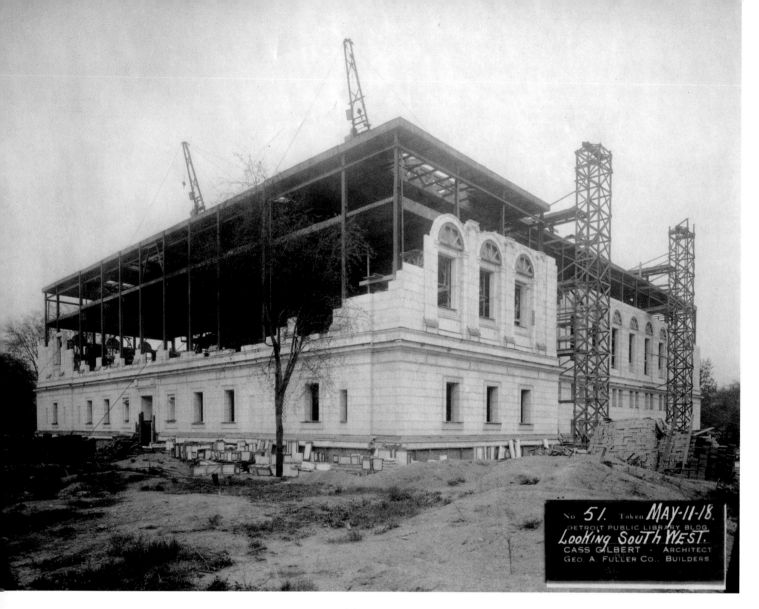

The framework continues to expand, May 11, 1918. Photograph by Charles Ruel Messinger. *Photograph courtesy of the Burton Historical Collection, Detroit Public Library.*

Stunning in its elegance, the Main Library upon completion, 1921.
Photograph courtesy of the Burton Historical Collection, Detroit Public Library.

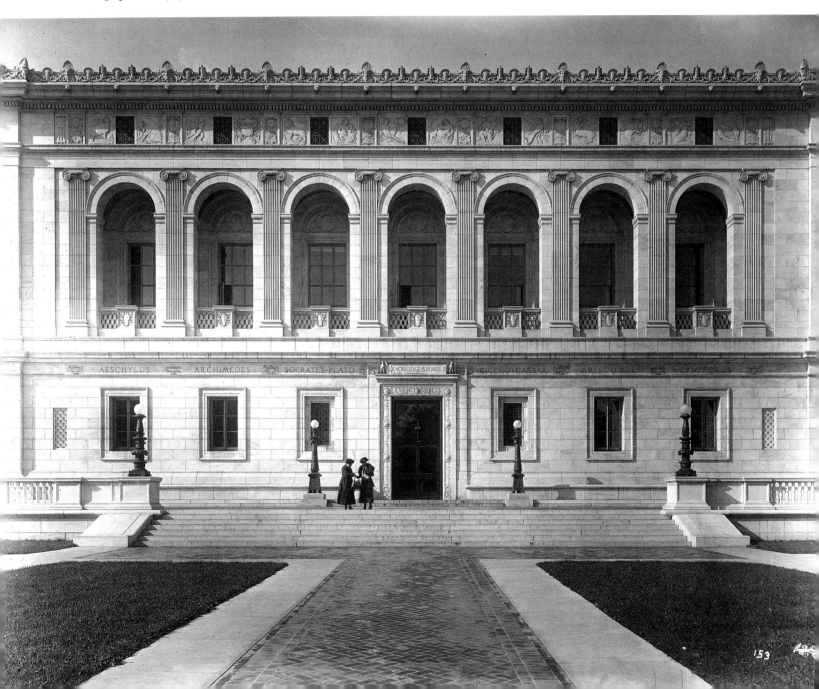

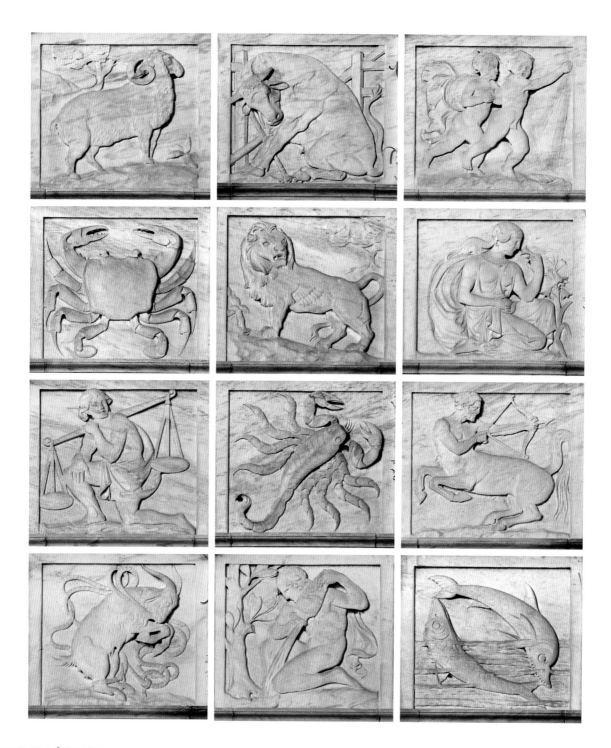

Incorporating classical design into the Main Library, Cass Gilbert created a mammoth frieze across the highest point of the facade depicting the twelve signs of the zodiac. Gilbert, along with Frederick J. Wiley, further utilized the signs of the zodiac on the painted windows located in the Delivery Room. From left to right the signs are: Aries (The Ram), Taurus (The Bull), Gemini (The Twins), Cancer (The Crab), Leo (The Lion), Virgo (The Virgin), Libra (The Scales), Scorpio (The Scorpion), Sagittarius (The Archer), Capricorn (The Mountain Sea Goat), Aquarius (The Water Bearer), and Pieces (The Fish). *Photographs courtesy of Jeff Morrison.*

Stonework on the upper facade features an ornate cornice, a frieze of zodiac representations, and three arches from the third-floor loggia. *Photograph courtesy of Kenneth Gabriel.*

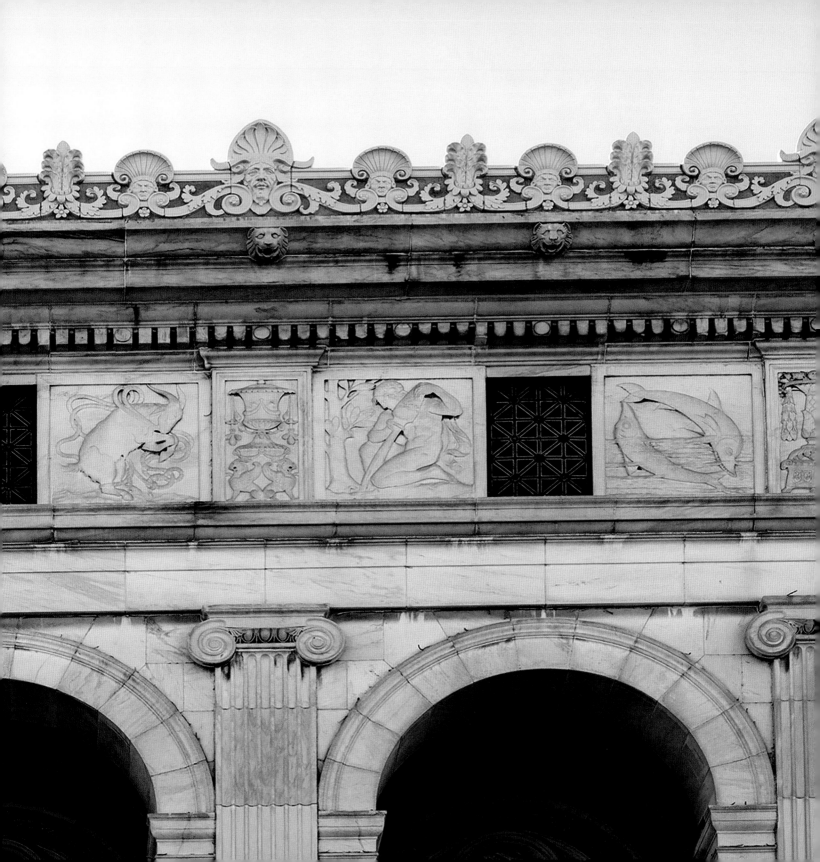

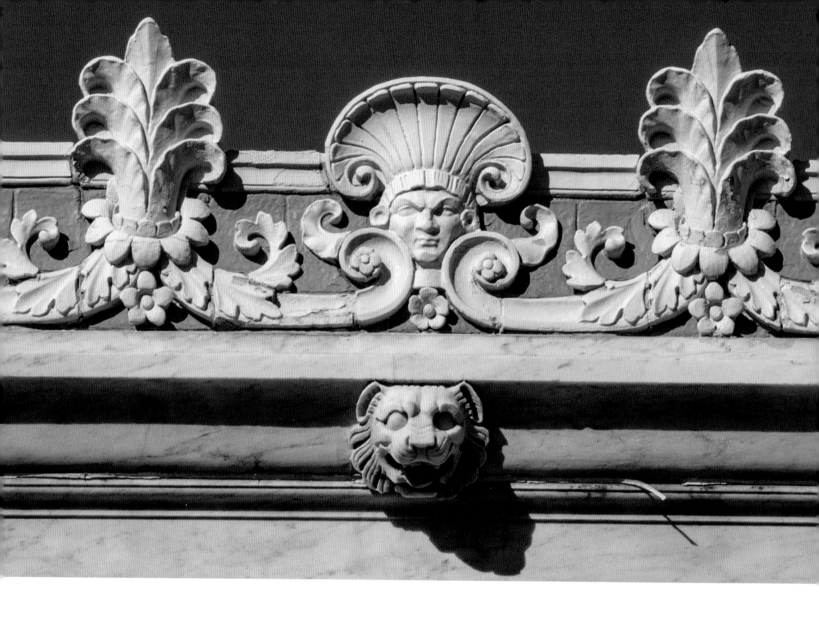

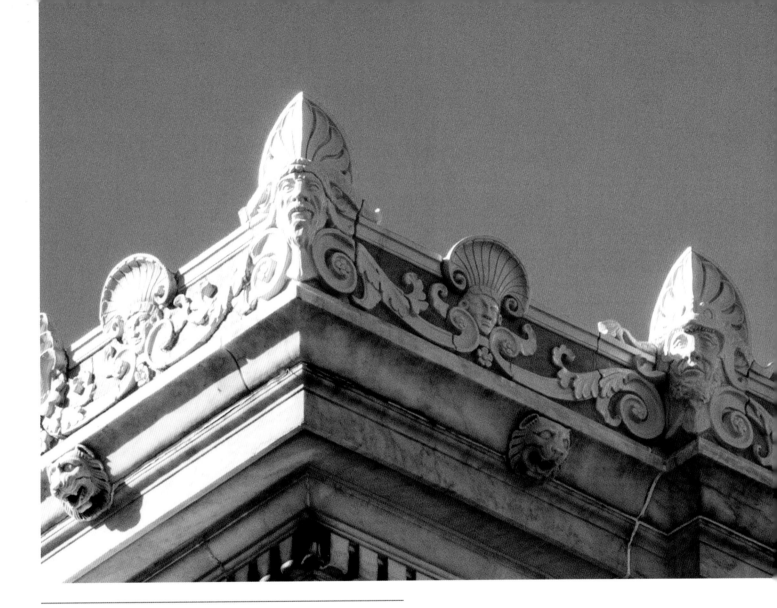

Executed by the Atlantic Terra Cotta Company, the cornice is colored with an old ivory tone backed with gold. Gilbert wanted the sun to radiate off the white marble facade, but he also wanted the facade to reflect the sun at the top of the building to draw the eye upward from the loggia. *Photograph courtesy of Kenneth Gabriel.*

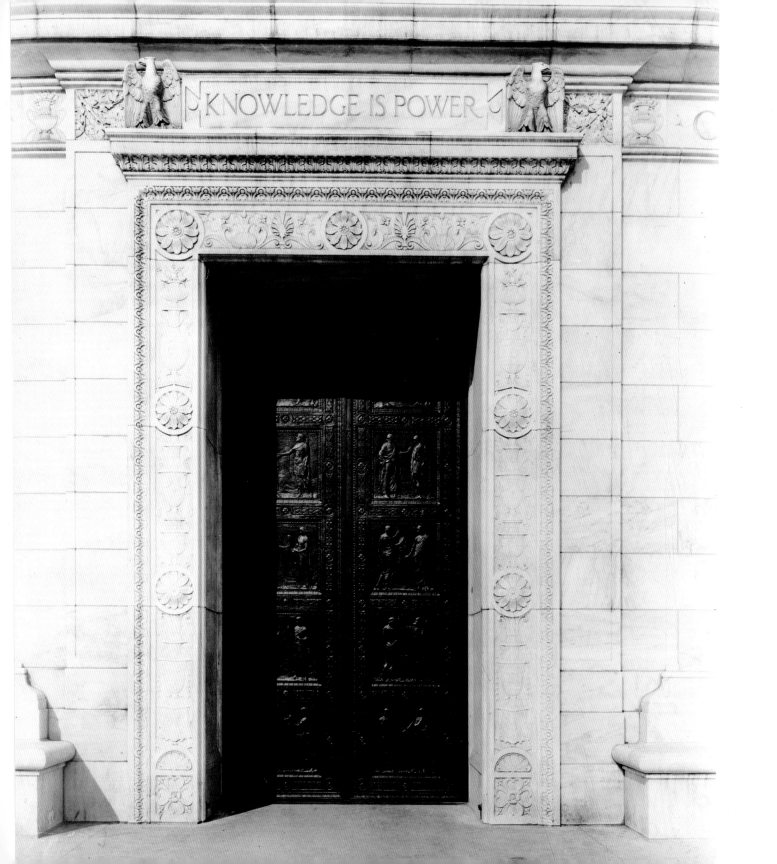

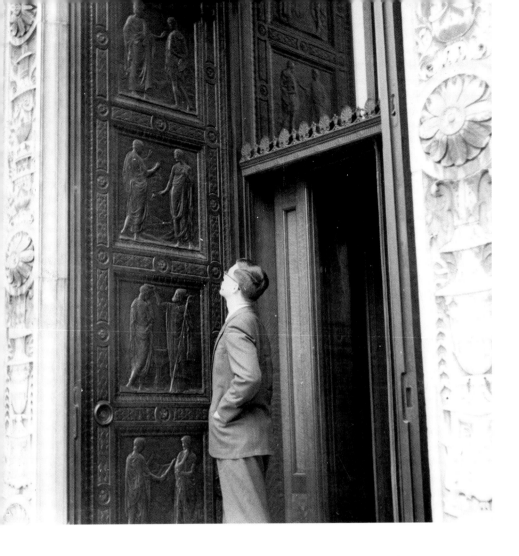

An unidentified gentleman studies a bronze doorway panel of a Roman teacher with his pupil. In a design that evokes Donatello's Sacristy doors in the Church of San Lorenzo, Florence, Italy, the doors were designed by John Donnelly Sr. and executed by John Polachek Bronze and Iron, New York. Over 15 feet tall, the doors are in bas-relief. *Photograph courtesy of the Burton Historical Collection, Detroit Public Library.*

FACING PAGE: View of the decorative marble doorway and bronze entrance doors to the Detroit Public Library. Note statement inscribed over door lintel: "Knowledge Is Power." *Photograph courtesy of the Burton Historical Collection, Detroit Public Library.*

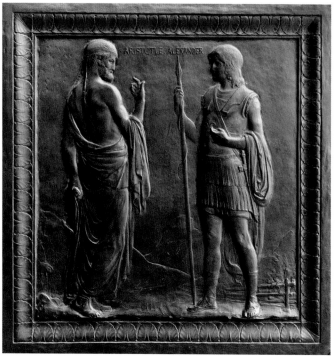

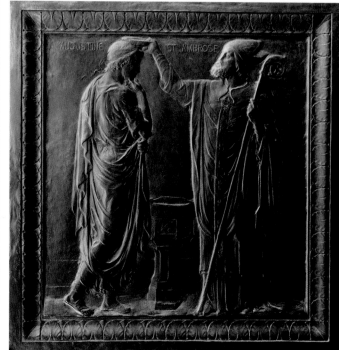

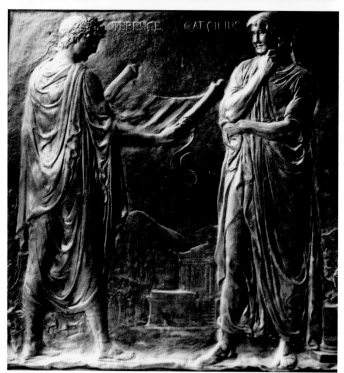

TOP LEFT: Aristotle walking with the young Alexander. *Photograph courtesy of Martin Vecchio.*

TOP RIGHT: The baptism of Augustine by St. Ambrose. *Photograph courtesy of Sam Sklar.*

BOTTOM RIGHT: Terence and Caccilius. *Photograph courtesy of the Burton Historical Collection, Detroit Public Library.*

The bronze door panels depict the phases of Greek and Roman literature: Epic, Tragic, Lyric, Philosophic, and Comic:

GRECIAN

Epic
Homer, as blind bard reciting
epic poetry

Tragic
Reception of Aeschylus at the
court of Hiero, King of Sicily

Lyric
Sappho teaching maidens of
her school

Philosophic
Aristotle walking with the
young Alexander

Comic
Aristophanes teaching the
young actor

ROMAN

Epic
Virgil receiving honors from the
Emperor Augustine

Tragic
Seneca teaching the young
Emperor Nero (age fourteen)

Lyric
Horace reading his works
to Maccenas

Philosophic
The baptism of Augustine by
St. Ambrose

Comic
Terence reading his first play
to Caccilius

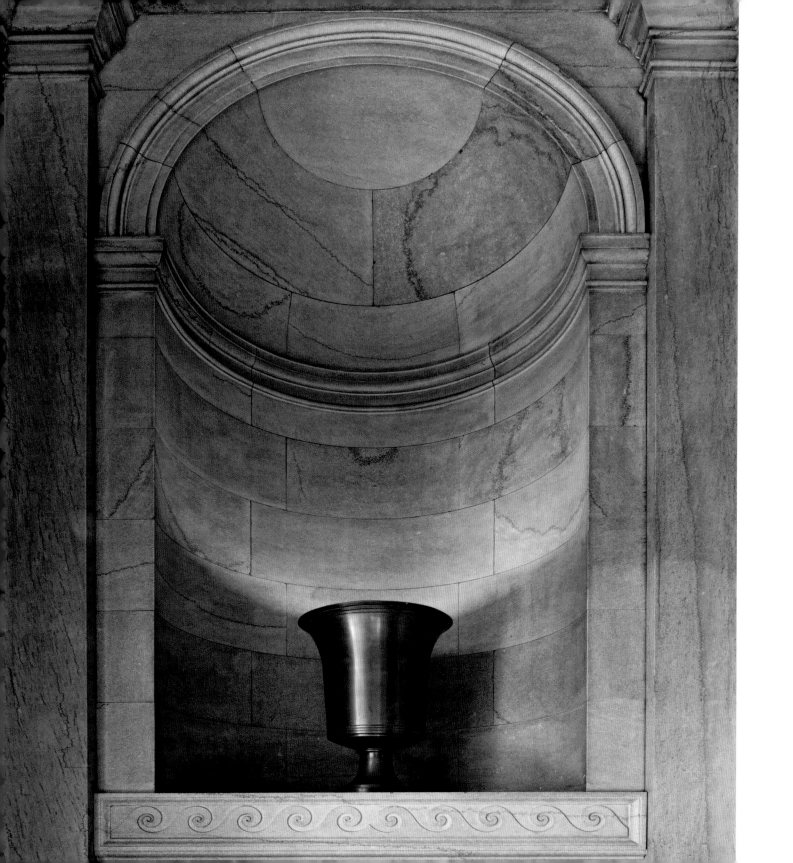

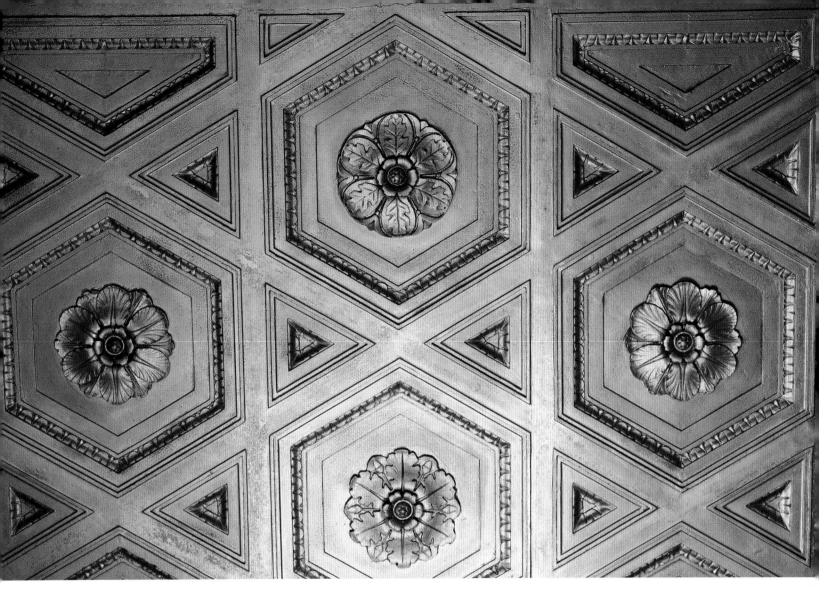

The gold-leaf ceiling of the vestibule features rosettes, hexagons, and triangular shapes. *Photograph courtesy of John Campbell.*

FACING PAGE: Upon entering the building, a small vestibule with two niches showcases lighted bronze urns. *Photograph courtesy of John Campbell.*

RIGHT: A colonnade of pink Tennessee marble adorns the Entrance Hall. *Photograph courtesy of Martin Vecchio.*

BELOW: Rosette in coffered panel is surrounded by Greek key design. *Photograph courtesy of Timothy Griffin.*

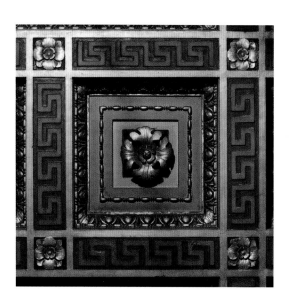

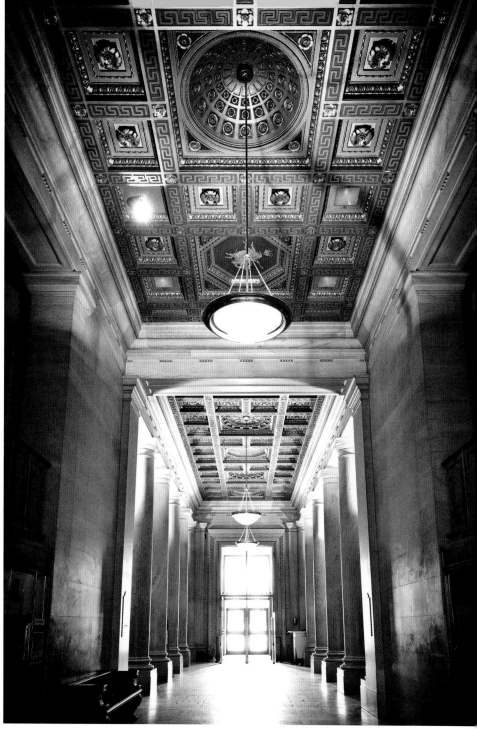

Children's Room

The Entrepreneur: Mary Chase Perry Stratton (1867–1961)

Mary Chase Perry Stratton was a pioneer in the American Arts and Crafts Movement and had an important role in the growth of ceramics. Stratton was born in 1867 in Hancock, Michigan, located in what is known as the Upper Peninsula's copper mining country. The origin of the name "Pewabic" is believed to have roots in the Chippewa word "wabic," which means metal, or "bewabic," which means iron or steel. It is also the name of a mine close to Stratton's childhood home.

Stratton began her art studies at the Art School of the Detroit Museum of Art. From 1887 to 1889 when she was in her early twenties, Stratton studied at the Cincinnati Art Academy in Ohio. Being an independent spirit in a man's field, she broke away from traditional china painting and became known for her signature iridescent glazes and large-scale installations. In 1903 Stratton, along with partner Horace James Caulkins, established a studio in a vacant house on Alfred Street in Detroit. They called it "The Stable Studio." In 1907, Pewabic moved to its new home on Jefferson Avenue where it continues to operate as a working studio.

Her inspiration was expressed in a 1932 interview with the *Detroit News* in which she shared an article titled "Develop the Resources of America." The article outlined the rich possibilities in soil for making the clays for pottery. Stratton explained, "Ever since I have been trying to develop the resources of America by using clays found in our soil."

Pewabic Pottery works can be found throughout Michigan and the United States. Noteworthy Michigan examples include the Detroit

Institute of Art, the Detroit Zoo, the Detroit Public Library, the Guardian Building, Detroit People Mover stations, the Buhl Building, Comerica Park, Holy Redeemer Church, St. Paul Cathedral, Christ Church at Cranbrook, and the Stephen M. Ross School of Business and Hill Auditorium on the campus of the University of Michigan, Ann Arbor. Pewabic Pottery can also be found in the Shedd Aquarium in Chicago, the Nebraska State Capital Building, and the Basilica of the National Shrine of the Immaculate Conception and the Freer Gallery at the Smithsonian Institute, both in Washington, D.C.

WORKS:
Loggia ceiling
Fireplace
Vases

THE CERMACIST:
HORACE JAMES CAULKINS (1850–1923)

Horace James Caulkins was born in Ontario, Canada, on July 25, 1850. In 1871, Caulkins moved to Detroit and worked in a dry goods business. In 1877, he began working as a dental supplier and in doing so developed a kiln for firing dental enamel. He invented what he called the Revelation: a kiln for firing dental enamel that would immensely impact his trade.

In 1903, Caulkins formed a partnership with Mary Chase Perry and began applying his Revelation technology with her understanding of glazes to ceramics. Their unique glazing technique placed Pewabic Pottery at the forefront of the field of American ceramics.

WORKS:
Loggia ceiling
Fireplace
Vases

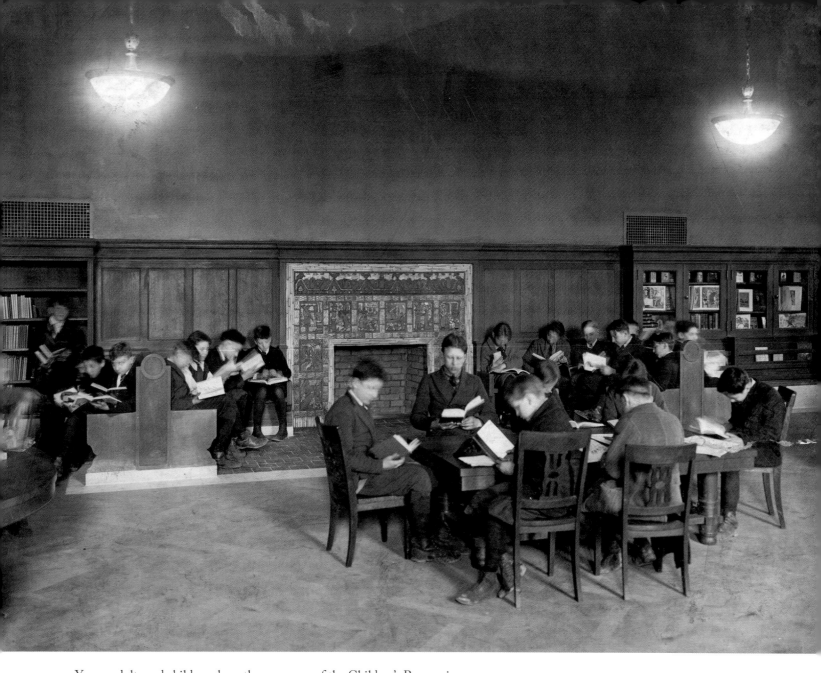

Young adults and children share the resources of the Children's Room, circa 1922. The Frederick J. Wiley map of Michigan and the Great Lakes was not yet installed. *Photograph courtesy of the Burton Historical Collection, Detroit Public Library.*

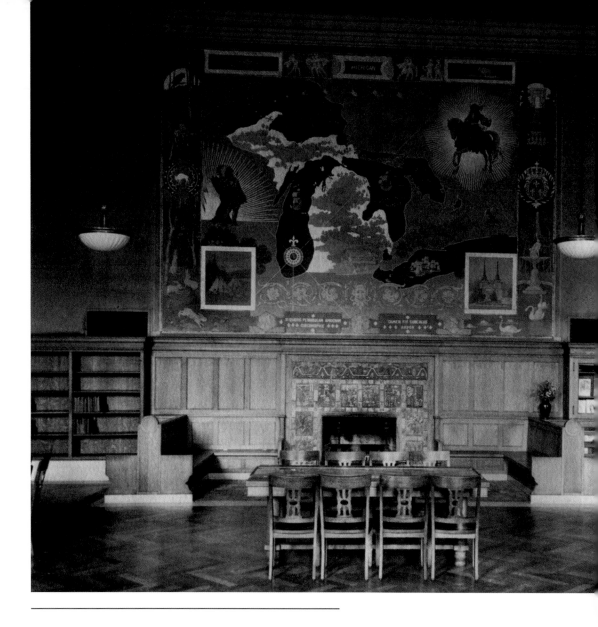

An undated picture of the original Children's Room with a
view of the wall map of Michigan and the Pewabic Pottery
fireplace. *Photograph courtesy of the Burton Historical
Collection, Detroit Public Library.*

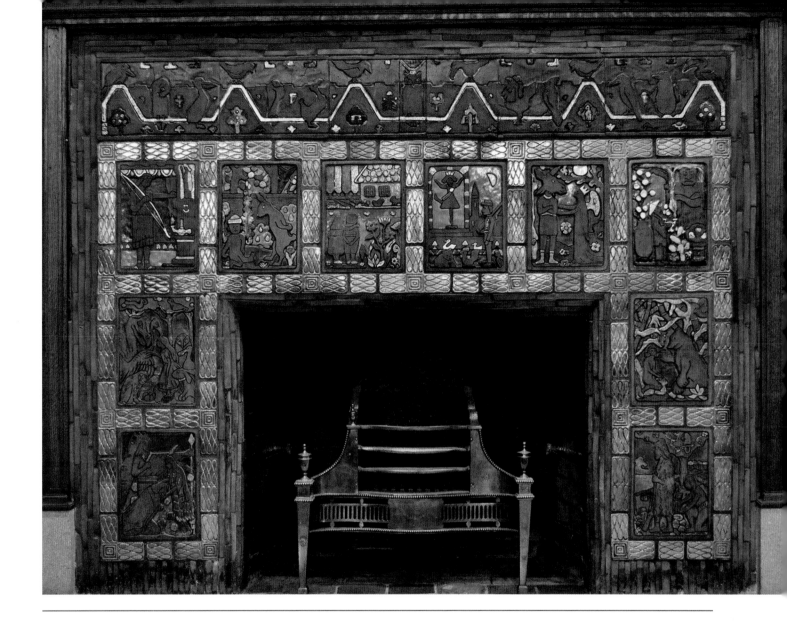

The Pewabic Fireplace designed and executed by Stratton and Caulkins depicting fairy tales and children's fables. Installed in 1920 at a cost of $525, the frieze illustrates the Aesop fable *The Owl and the Birds*. The subjects of the tiles are (*bottom, left to right*) Pocahontas and John Smith, Alice in Wonderland, Ulysses, Tar Baby and Br'er Rabbit, Hansel and Gretel, the Tin Solider, Titania and Bottom, Aladdin, Mowgli and the Bear, and Robinson Crusoe. *Photograph courtesy of Paul Erickson.*

FOLLOWING PAGES: Pewabic Fireplace detail of tiles. *Left to right*: Hansel and Gretel, the Tin Soldier, and Titania and Bottom from *A Midsummer Night's Dream*. Note iridescent glaze unique to Pewabic. *Photographs courtesy of Timothy Griffin.*

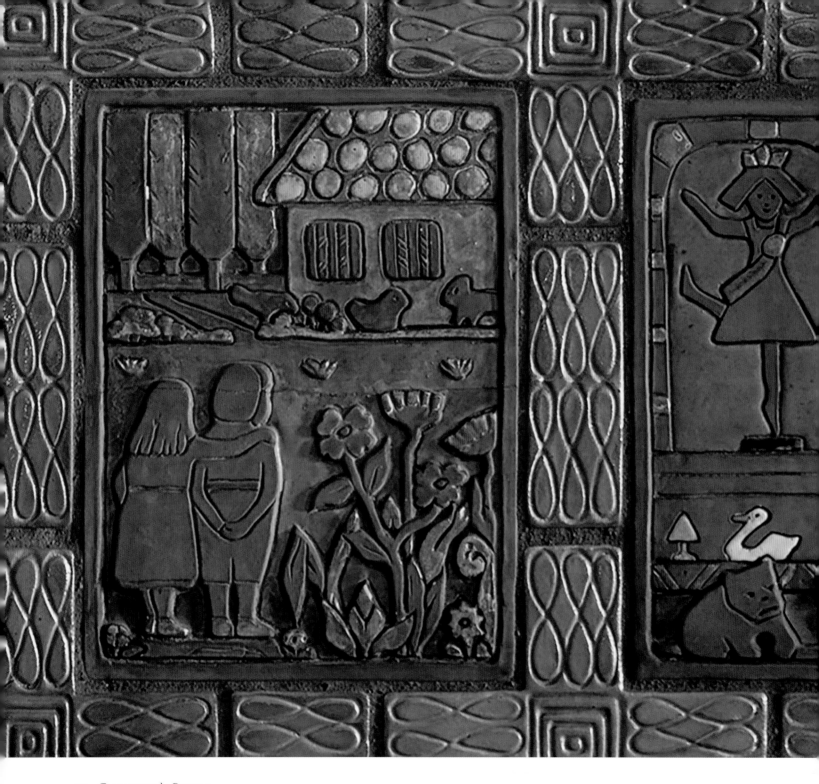

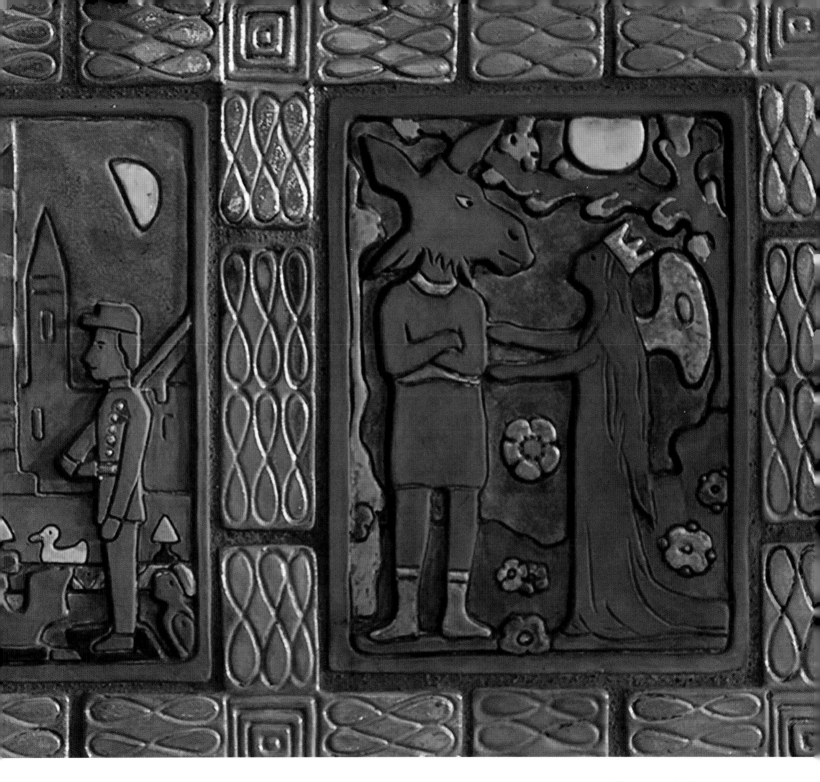

When children are taught by this process, geography becomes a joy.

FRANKLYN PARIS, COMMENTING ON
FREDERICK J. WILEY'S MAP, 1925

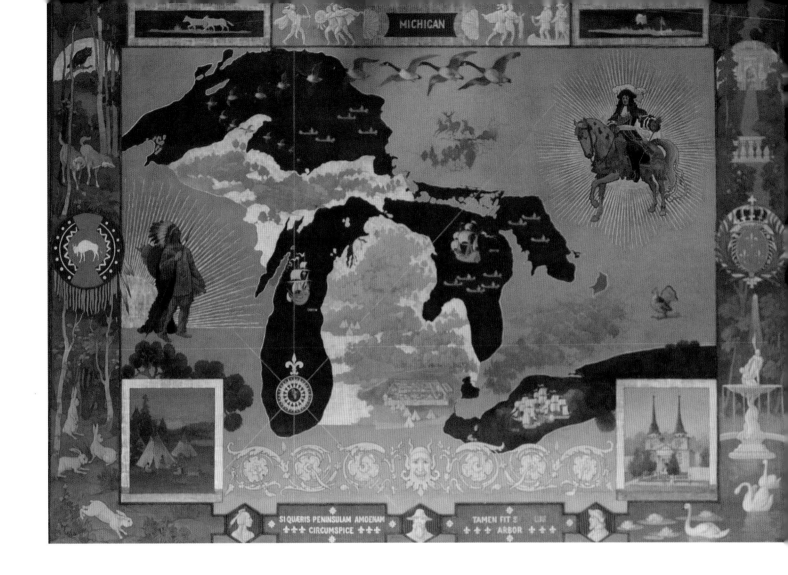

Pictorial map of Michigan designed by Frederick J. Wiley for the Children's Room. At the base of the map are two Latin quotes:

Si Quaeris Peninsulman Amoenam Circumspice (If you seek a pleasant peninsula, look about you.)   —motto of the State of Michigan

Tamen Fit Surculus Arbor (The shoot at length becomes a tree.)   —motto of Michigan while it was a territory

Photograph courtesy of Timothy Griffin.

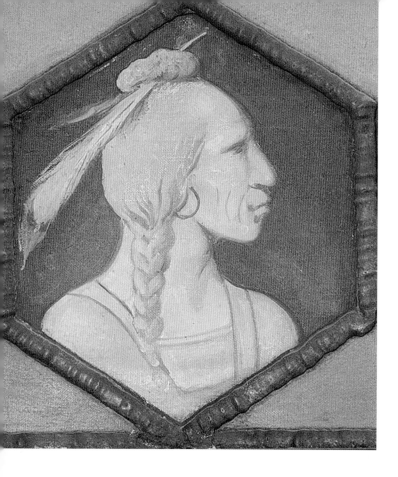

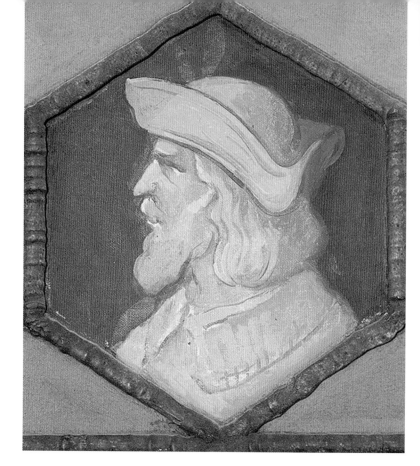

ABOVE LEFT: Small medallion of Iroquois brave adorns lower left border of map.

ABOVE RIGHT: Medallion of the explorer La Salle, who visited the site of Detroit in 1670.

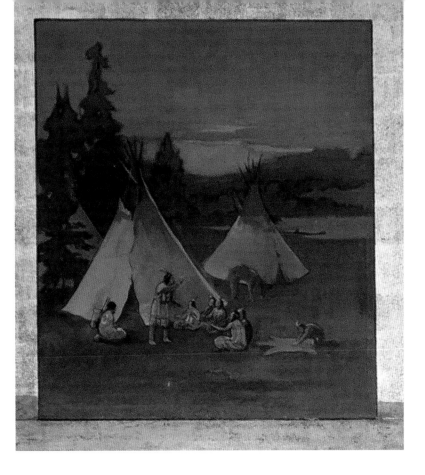

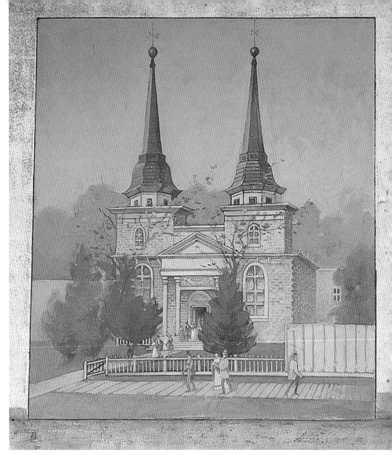

ABOVE LEFT: On the left corner of the map, an Indian encampment.

Photographs courtesy of Timothy Griffin.

ABOVE RIGHT: In small frame, the Church of St. Anne, Detroit, lower right.

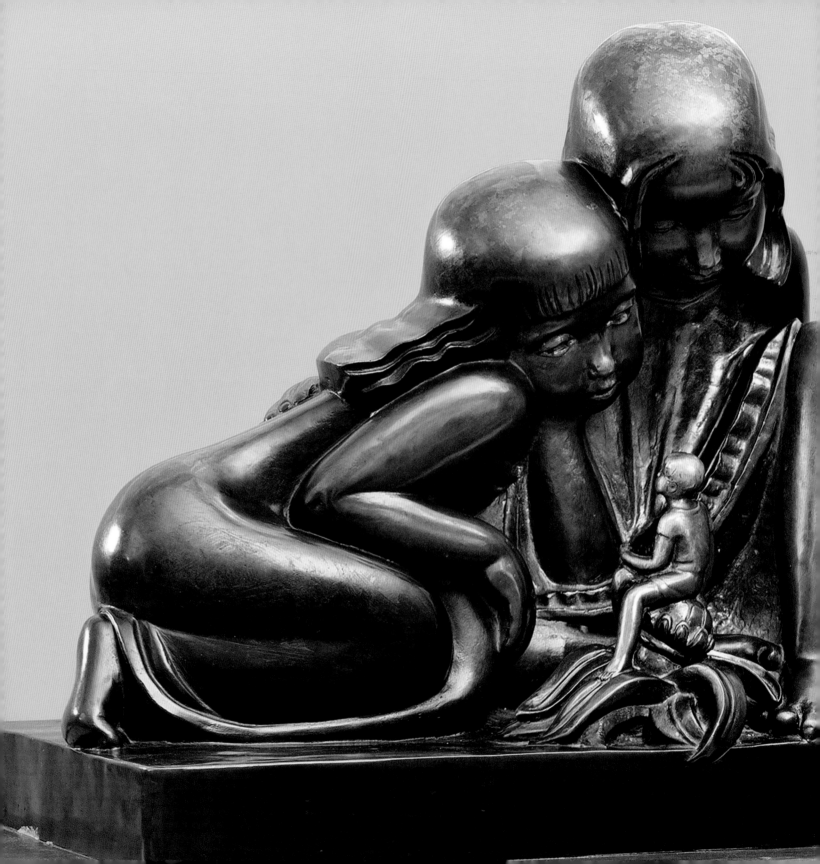

SAMUEL CASHWAN (1899–1988)

Samuel Cashwan was born in Cherkassy, Russia, in 1899 and immigrated with his family to New York in 1905, moving to Detroit in 1916. His father was a cabinet maker and house builder. Samuel exhibited a strong interest in art at an early age. The family settled in Detroit in 1916. Cashwan left Detroit to study at the Architectural League of New York and the École des Beaux-Arts in Paris. Upon returning to Detroit in 1927, he worked as an art instructor at the University of Michigan, served as the head of the sculpture department of the Detroit Society of Arts and Crafts, and was hired as a designer by General Motors Corporation.

From 1936 to 1942 Cashwan was employed by the Works Progress Administration (WPA) as the supervisor of the Michigan Sculpture and Ceramics Program. Cashwan's stylized and abstract sculptures decorate many public buildings throughout Michigan including the *Brady Memorial* on Belle Isle, Detroit (1928), *Abraham Lincoln* in Augusta Township (1938), *Pioneer Mother* in Clare (1938), *Three Musicians* at Michigan State University, East Lansing (1940), and the *Miller Memorial* at the Kellogg Building at the University of Michigan, Ann Arbor (1940). Other noteworthy works include *A Woman* at the Detroit Institute of Arts and reliefs at St. Aloysius Church and the Edwin Denby Memorial in Detroit.

The Adventures of Tom Thumb, 1936, by Samuel Cashwan. Two children are mesmerized by Tom Thumb sitting atop a flower. WPA Commission, cast bronze, 20 inches high. Gift to the Detroit Public Library in memory of children's librarian Elizabeth Knapp. *Photograph courtesy of Martin Vecchio.*

GRAND STAIRCASE

THE AMERICAN MURALISTS

EDWIN HOWLAND BLASHFIELD (1848–1936)

Born in New York City in 1848, Edwin Howland Blashfield studied engineering at the Massachusetts Institute of Technology. His artistic education began at the Pennsylvania Academy of the Fine Arts, followed by study abroad in Paris with the French academic painters Leon Bonnat and Jean-Leon Gerome. Initially interested in easel painting, he changed his focus to illustration, and he ultimately focused on public art through mural painting. A pivotal moment in his career came when he was asked to paint the dome in the Manufacturer's and Liberal Arts building at the 1893 World's Columbian Exposition held in Chicago.

Within the double Grand Staircase of the Detroit Public Library are five murals created by Blashfield. In depicting significant figures throughout art history, he had one goal in mind: to inspire the quest for knowledge. He carefully organized the compositions to lead one's eyes across the painter's surface to inspire the ideas of universal truths. In addition to being an accomplished writer and lecturer, Blashfield was considered one of the most notable American muralists of his day. His works decorated high-profile public and commercial buildings throughout the United States.

His classic training profoundly influenced his approach to mural painting. Using the principles of composition, perspective, color, scale, proportion, rhythm, and pattern, Blashfield understood the importance of integrating the art into the architectural space, particularly with regard to public art. The collaboration between the muralist, architect, decorator, and patron was critical to the grand expression of his art. He cautioned against painting based on what he considered trivial subjects or those not having the noble aspirations for public buildings. He believed in representing classical beauty and traditional subjects of moral significance.

Some of his significant works can be found in the Minnesota and Wisconsin state capitals; the Federal Courthouse in Baltimore, Maryland; the Grand Ballroom of the Waldorf-Astoria Hotel, Appellate Courthouse, and William K. Vanderbilt residence in New York City; the mosaic of St. Matthew in Saint Matthew's Cathedral; and the dome of the main reading room of the Thomas Jefferson building of the Library of Congress in Washington, D.C.

A serious academic artist, Blashfield served as the president of the Society of American Artists (1865–96), a member of the National Institute of Arts and Letters (1914–16), and president of the National Academy of Design (1920–26). A respected writer, he translated Vasari's *Lives of the Painter* (four volumes, 1897) and published *Mural Painting in America* in 1913.

WORKS:
Grand Staircase murals, 1922

OIL ON CANVAS:
The Poets
Music
The Joining of the Ways
Graphic Arts
Prose

Vincent Aderente (1880–1941)

Born in Naples, Italy, and arriving in the United States with his parents at the age of eight, Vincent Aderente spent most of his childhood exploring the Metropolitan Museum of Art and copying the great paintings. At seventeen, he received the Scholarship Prize, the Money Prize, the Illustrator's Prize, and the Composition Prize at the Student's Art League. His artistic creativity was recognized by Edwin Howland Blashfield, who in 1897 asked Aderente to assist him in creating mural decorations. Their collaboration continued for more than twenty years.

Aderente later established a studio in New York City and one at his home in Bayside, New York. A prolific artist of public art, he was also a remarkable illustrator. He created a host of covers for the *American Weekly* and *Motor Magazine* in addition to illustrated poems. Aderente was a true American patriot, designing savings bonds for the United States Postal Service and a famous World War I poster titled "Columbia Calls."

Some of Aderentes's most notable works include the Grand Staircase murals at the Detroit Public Library, the ceiling and proscenium of the Boston Opera House (originally the Keith Memorial Theatre), three lunettes in the United States Mint in Denver, two murals in the Queens Supreme Courthouse in Jamaica, New York, and fifty-seven cameo portraits in the foyer of the Luzerne County Courthouse in Wilkes-Barre, Pennsylvania.

WORKS:
Grand Staircase murals, 1922

OIL ON CANVAS:
The Poets
Music
The Joining of the Ways
Graphic Arts
Prose

I am deeply interested in the improvement of art work in public buildings.

Vincente Aderente

FACING PAGE: The Grand Staircase, Main Library. Note the painted glass window and barrel-vaulted ceiling. The mural *The Poets* rises above. *Photograph courtesy of Martin Vecchio.*

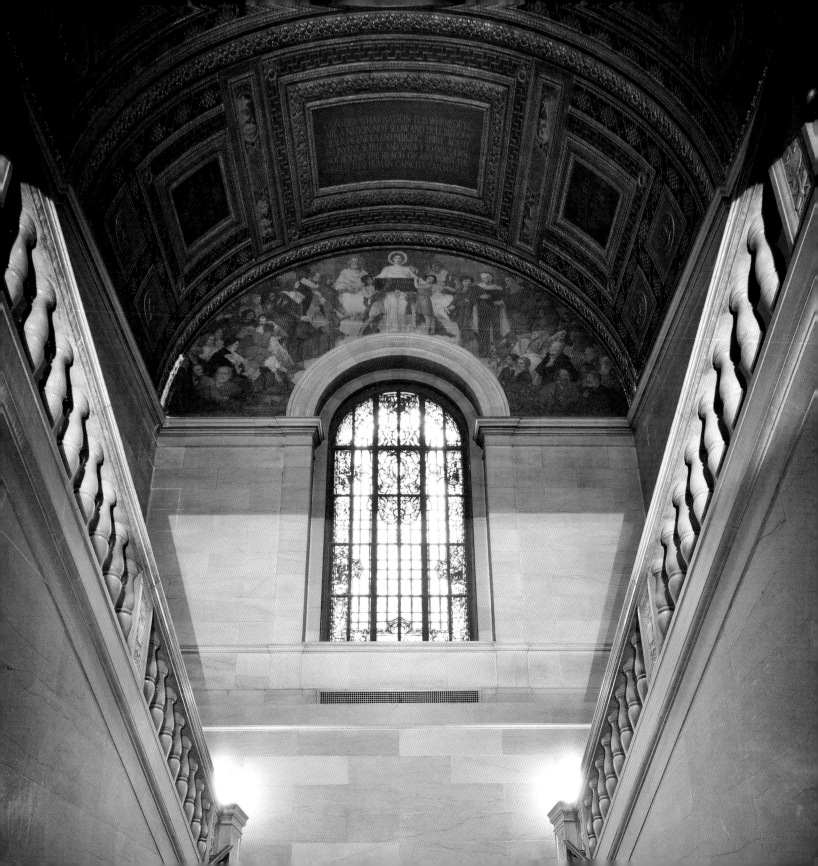

Painted glass window stating "Labor Vinces" (through labor you will conquer) with panels depicting individuals in their pursuit of the arts. *Photographs courtesy of Timothy Griffin.*

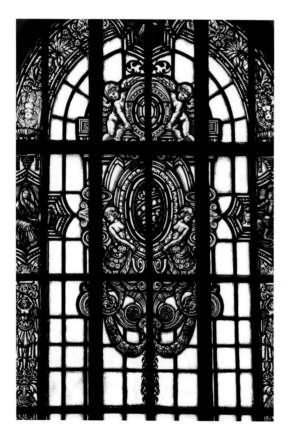

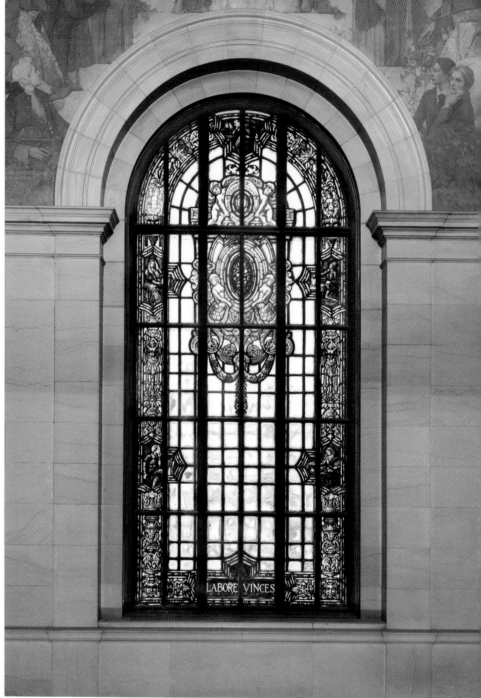

Barrel-vaulted ceiling of the Grand Staircase. *Photograph courtesy of Buchanan House Photography.*

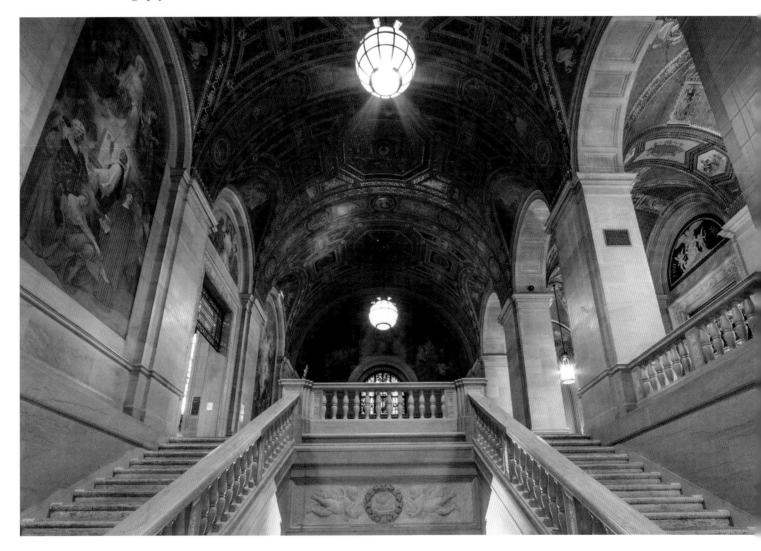

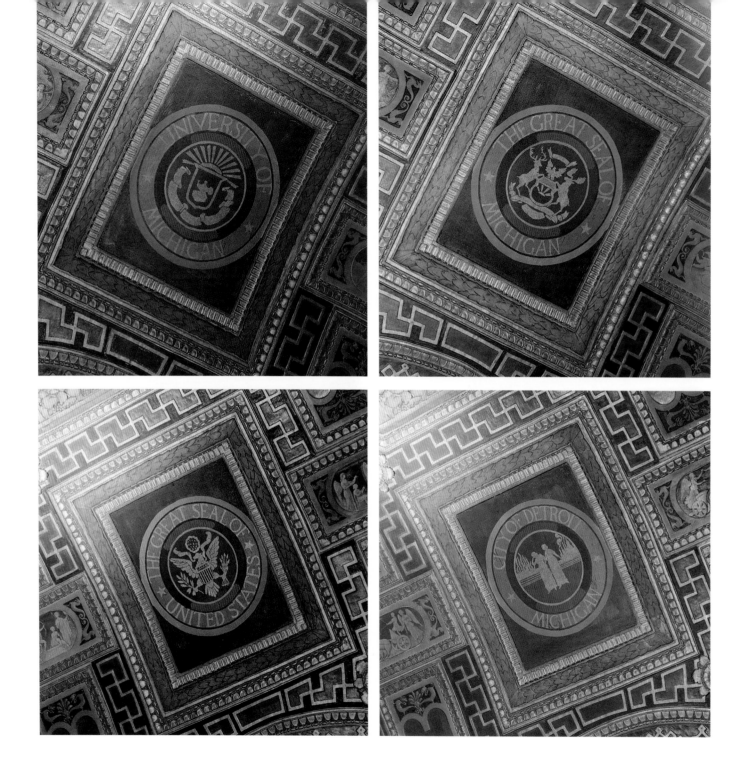

In adorning the barrel vaulted ceiling over the Grand Staircase, Wiley showcased his interpretations of four notable seals: the *University of Michigan Seal*, the *Great Seal of the State of Michigan*, the *Great Seal of the United States*, and the *Great Seal of the City of Detroit*. *Photographs courtesy of John Campbell.*

TOP LEFT: *University of Michigan Seal.* Earlier versions of the seal were created when the University was founded in Detroit in 1817. Wiley's interpretation replicates the 1837 seal when the University was relocated to Ann Arbor. The significance of the "lamp of knowledge" is obvious. The rising sun atop the shield is derived from the coat of arms of the State of Michigan.

TOP RIGHT: *Great Seal of the State of Michigan.* Designed by Lewis Cass and adopted in 1835, the seal features a coat of arms of the State of Michigan on a light-blue field. On a dark-blue shield the sun rises over a lake and a peninsula, and a man holding a long gun with a raised hand represents peace and the ability to defend his rights. The elk and moose are symbols of Michigan, while the bald eagle represents the United States.

BOTTOM LEFT: *Great Seal of the United States.* The design on the obverse (or front) of the seal is depicted in the library. The shield is different from the American flag in two ways: first, it has no stars on the blue chief, and second, the outermost stripes are white, not red, so as not to violate the heraldic rule of tincture.

The supporter of the shield is a bald eagle with its wings outstretched (or "splayed," in heraldic terms). The eagle holds a bundle of thirteen arrows in its left talon, referring to the thirteen original states, and an olive branch in its right talon, together symbolizing that the United States has "a strong desire for peace, but will always be ready for war." The eagle has its head turned toward the olive branch, on its right side, said to symbolize a preference for peace. In its beak, the eagle clutches a scroll with the motto *E pluribus unum* (out of many, one). Over its head there appears a "glory" with thirteen mullets (stars) on a blue field arranged in rows of 1-4-3-4-1, forming a six-pointed star. The design was approved and the seal adopted in 1782.

BOTTOM RIGHT: *Great Seal of the City of Detroit.* The seal features two female figures, one representing Detroit when it burned down in 1805 and the other representing the modern-day Detroit that rose from the ashes, rebuilding and growing into a very successful city.

In the background are three lions, fleur-de-lis, red and white stripes, and thirteen stars. The fleur-de-lis are symbolic of the United States' French origins and the lions our British origins. The thirteen stars and red and white stripes represent the original thirteen colonies of the United States of America.

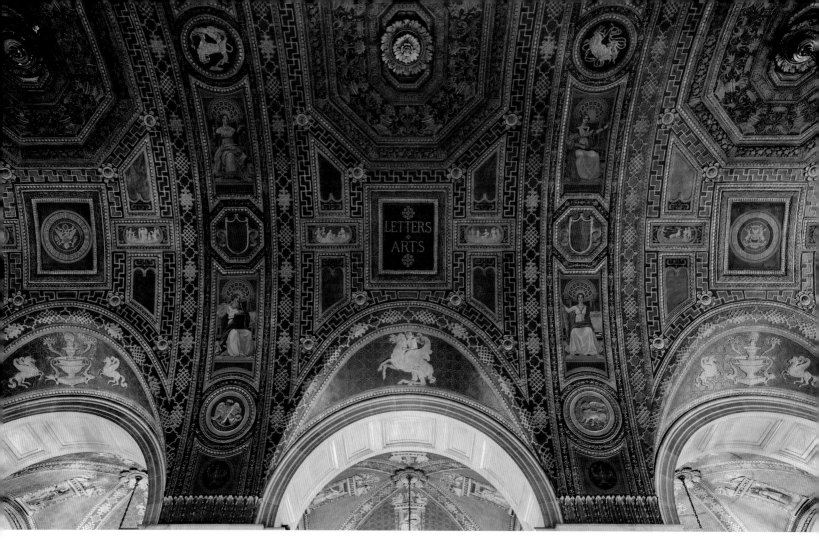

Wiley's stunning barrel-vaulted ceiling above the Grand Staircase. *Photograph courtesy of Sam Sklar.*

Two quotes in rectangular panels bear the following inscriptions: South end: "Consider what nation it is whereof ye are; a nation not slow and dull, but of a quick, ingenious and piercing spirit, acute to invent, subtle and sinuous to discourse, not beyond the reach of any point the highest that human capacity can soar to." North end: "Reading, trying all things, assenting to the force of reason and convincement; what wants there to such towardly and pregnant soil, but wise and faithful laborers to make a knowing people, a nation of profits, of sages, and of worthies."

Mural representing *The Poets. Photograph courtesy of Martin Vecchio.*

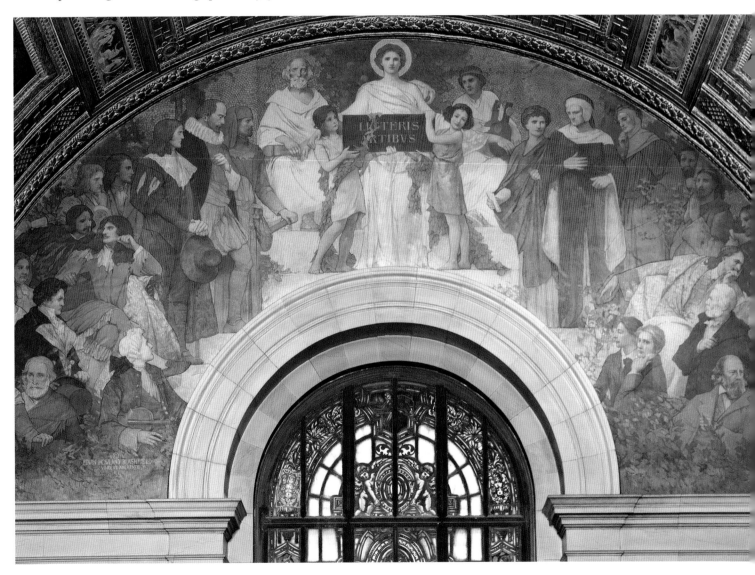

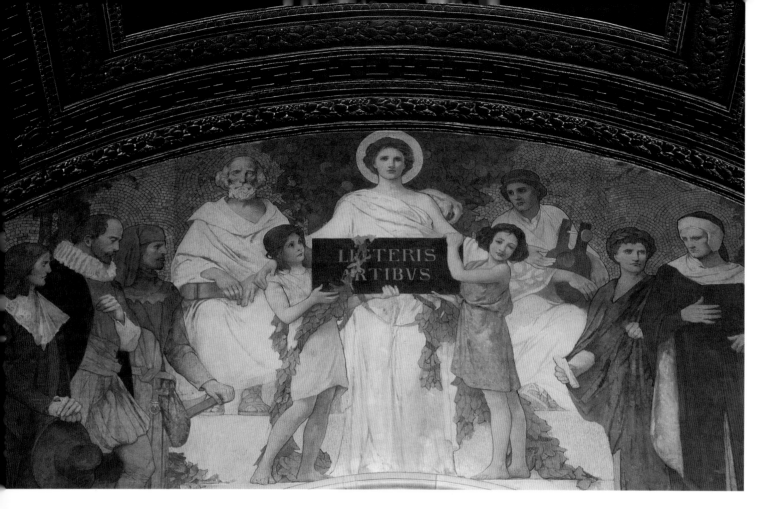

ABOVE: Letteris Artibvs. In the center stands a muse surrounded by two children holding an inscribed tablet. *Photograph courtesy of Timothy Griffin.*

FACING PAGE:

TOP: Guide to thirty-seven individuals portrayed in *The Poets*. Taken from Detroit Public Library, *Library Service Manual*, 1922.

BOTTOM: The mural over the opposing wall represents *Prose*. Guide to thirty-seven individuals pictured. Taken from the Detroit Public Library, *Library Service Manual*, 1922.

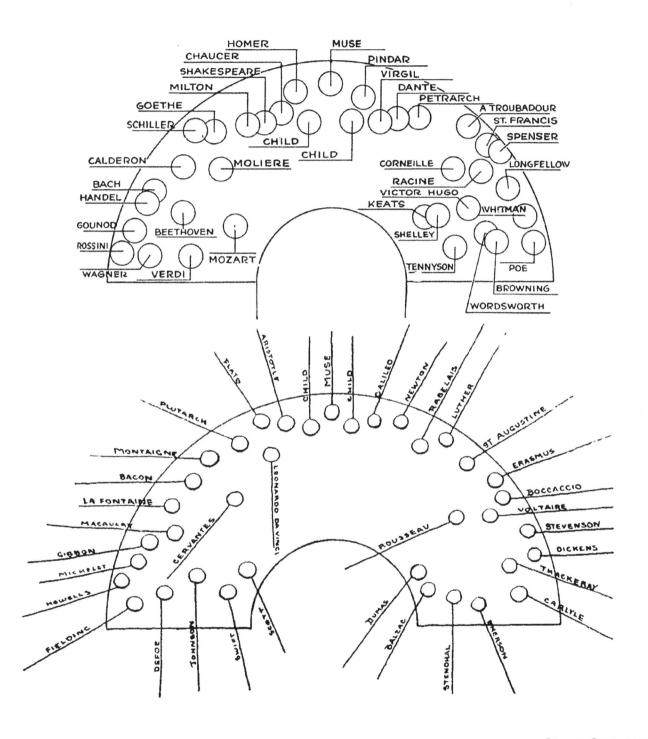

HOMER   MUSE
CHAUCER   PINDAR
SHAKESPEARE   VIRGIL
MILTON   DANTE
GOETHE   PETRARCH
SCHILLER   A TROUBADOUR
    ST. FRANCIS
    SPENSER
CALDERON   CHILD   CHILD   CORNEILLE   LONGFELLOW
    MOLIERE   RACINE
BACH   VICTOR HUGO
HANDEL   KEATS   WHITMAN
GOUNOD   BEETHOVEN   SHELLEY
ROSSINI   MOZART   POE
WAGNER   VERDI   TENNYSON
    WORDSWORTH   BROWNING

PLATO   ARISTOTLE   CHILD   MUSE   CHILD   GALILEO   NEWTON   RABELAIS   LUTHER
PLUTARCH   ST. AUGUSTINE
MONTAIGNE   ERASMUS
BACON   BOCCACCIO
LA FONTAINE   LEONARDO DA VINCI   VOLTAIRE
MACAULAY   STEVENSON
GIBBON   CERVANTES   ROUSSEAU   DICKENS
MICHELET   THACKERAY
HOWELLS   CARLYLE
FIELDING   DEFOE   JOHNSON   SWIFT   SCOTT   DUMAS   BALZAC   STENDHAL   EMERSON

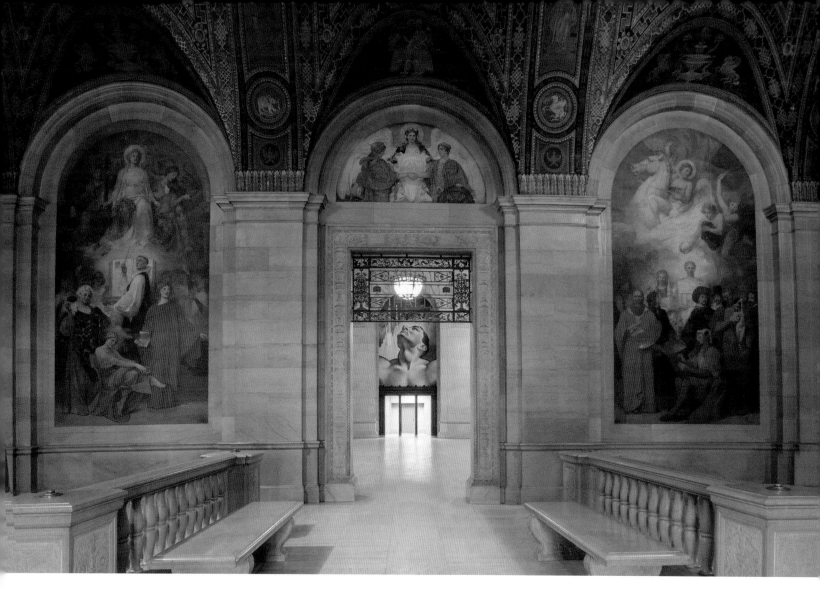

The three beautiful Blashfield and Aderente murals at the entrance to Adam Strohm Hall. *Photograph courtesy of Buchanan House Photography.*

Mural representing *Music*. At the top, the patron saint of music, St. Cecelia, is surrounded by two female musicians. In the middle, an ecclesiastic monk is surrounded by choir boys. A woman in red represents opera, a seated woman represents dance, and a woman with a mask depicts light opera or drama. *Photograph courtesy of Trista Dymond.*

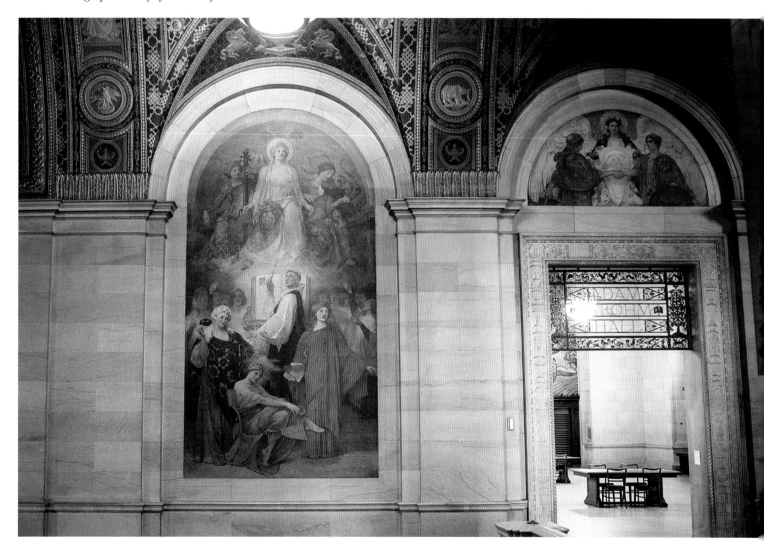

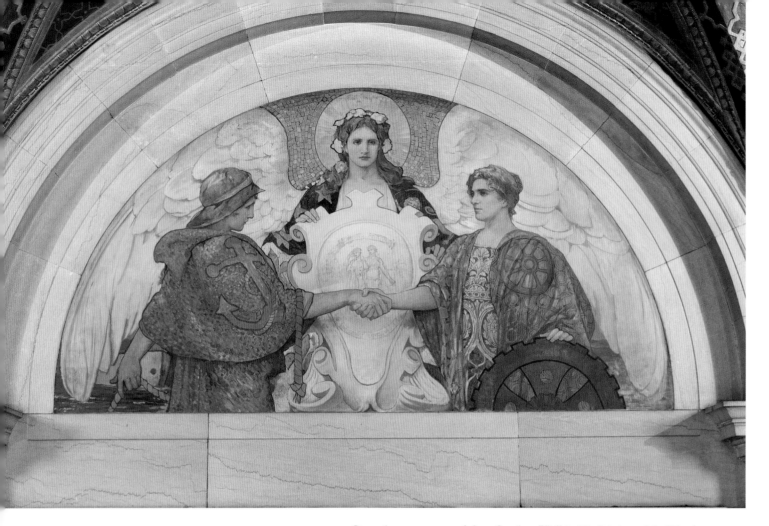

Over the entrance to Adam Strohm Hall is *The Joining of the Ways* by Blashfield and Aderente. The youthful figure on the left is adorned with a cape embossed with an anchor representing the Great Lakes waterways. The woman on the right holds a wheel representing industry. The central winged female figure represents youth and vitality and the spirit of Detroit. Her cape is adorned with imagery of the American flag and on her lap she holds a shield imprinted with the seal of the City of Detroit. *Photograph courtesy of Martin Vecchio.*

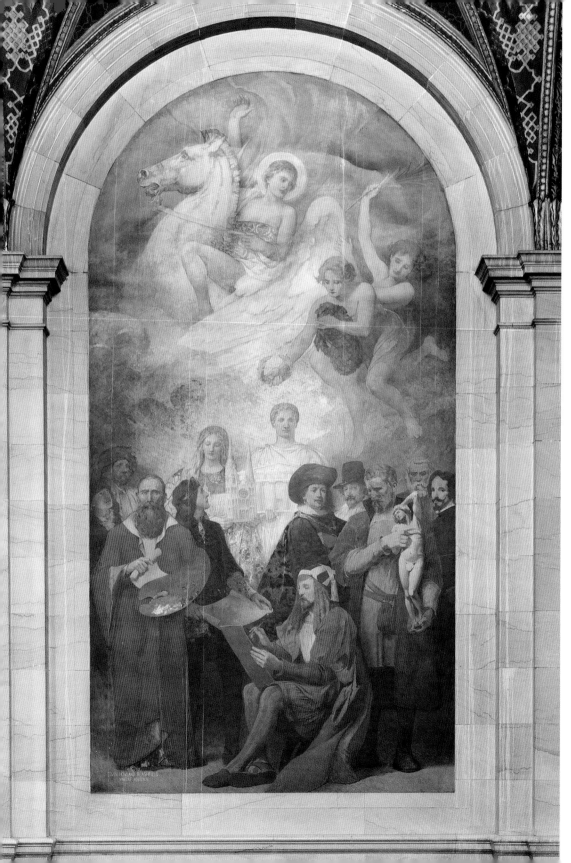

This mural by Blashfield and Aderente represents *The Graphic Arts*. In the center a man and a woman representing Greek and Gothic architecture hold models of the Parthenon and the Cathedral at Chartres. Above, a genius mounted on Pegasus flies upward. Two figures throw a wreath and palms down upon a group of artists. Standing from left to right: Giorgione, Donatello (in the background), Titian, Raphael, Rembrandt, Rubens, Michelangelo, Tintoretto (in background), Velasquez, and Durer (seated). *Photograph courtesy of Martin Vecchio.*

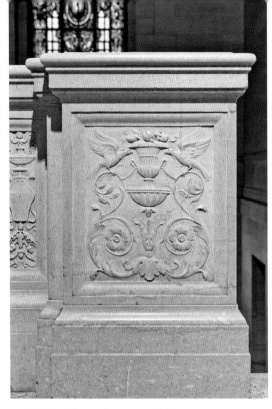

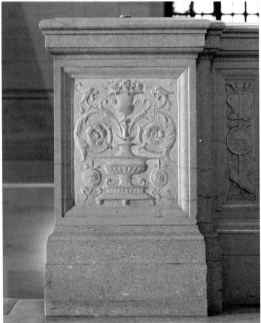

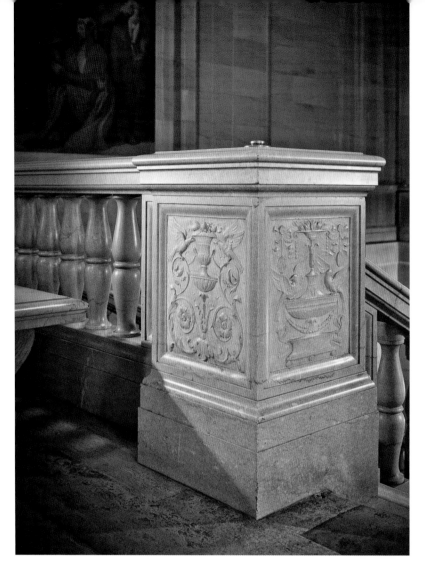

ABOVE: Decorative stonework adorns the column adjacent to the balustrade of the Grand Staircase. *Photograph courtesy of Martin Vecchio.*

LEFT, TOP: Birds with wings splayed with an urn of fruit adorned by acanthus leaves and rosettes. *Photograph courtesy of Martin Vecchio.*

LEFT, BOTTOM: Dragon-like faces flank an urn of fruit, surrounded by acanthus leaves. *Photograph courtesy of Martin Vecchio.*

Two putti or cherubs hold a lamp in one hand and a wreath in the other. Inside the wreath are books which symbolize knowledge and a lamp for enlightenment. *Photograph courtesy of John Campbell.*

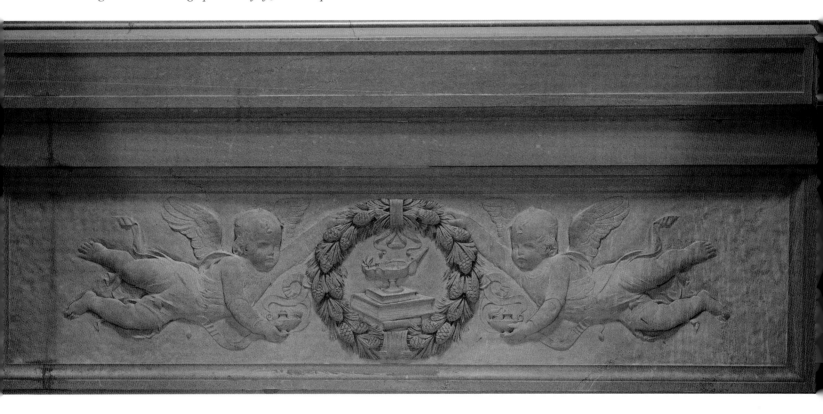

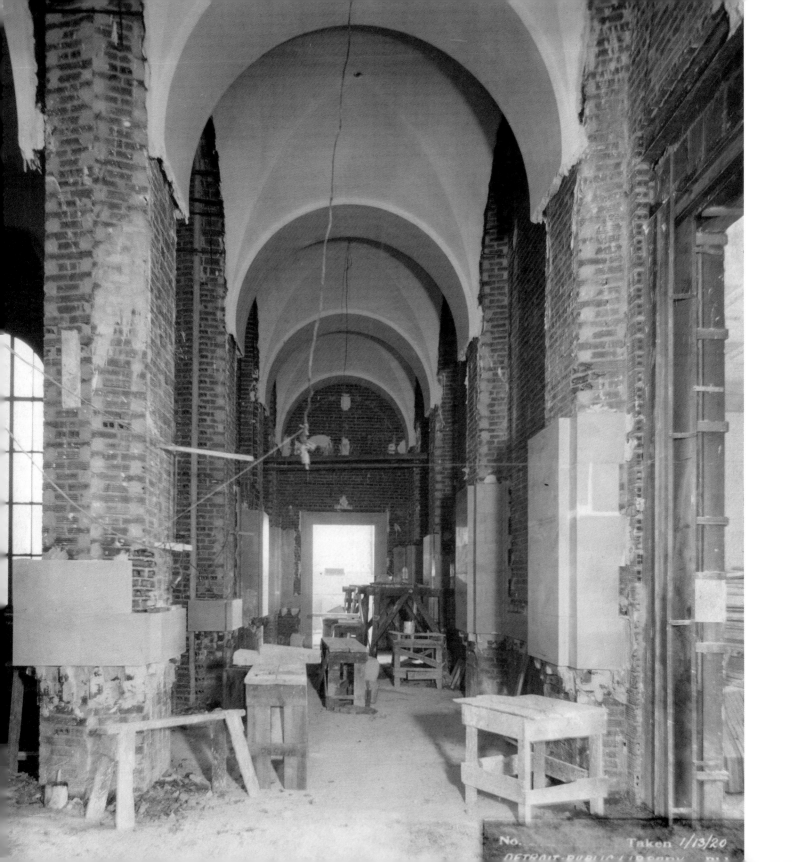

No.   Taken 1/13/20
DETROIT PUBLIC LIBRARY

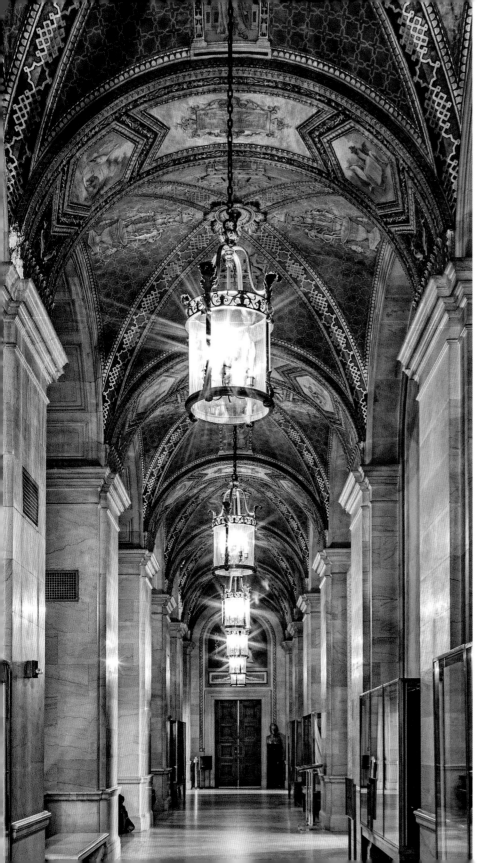

Wiley designed the ceiling with seven vaults intersected by arches decorated with features from Aesop's Fables. Additional allegorical figures are depicted, representing architecture, painting, tragedy, astronomy, and theology. *Photograph courtesy of Pat Eisenberger.*

FACING PAGE: View of the arched corridor on the third floor, July 1920. *Photograph courtesy of the Burton Historical Collection, Detroit Public Library.*

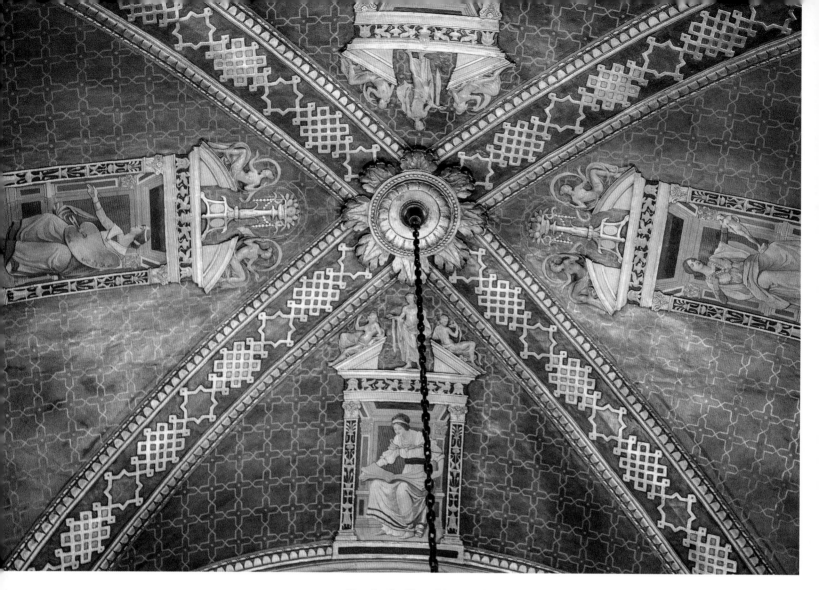

Detail of ceiling. *Photograph courtesy of Joy VanBuhler.*

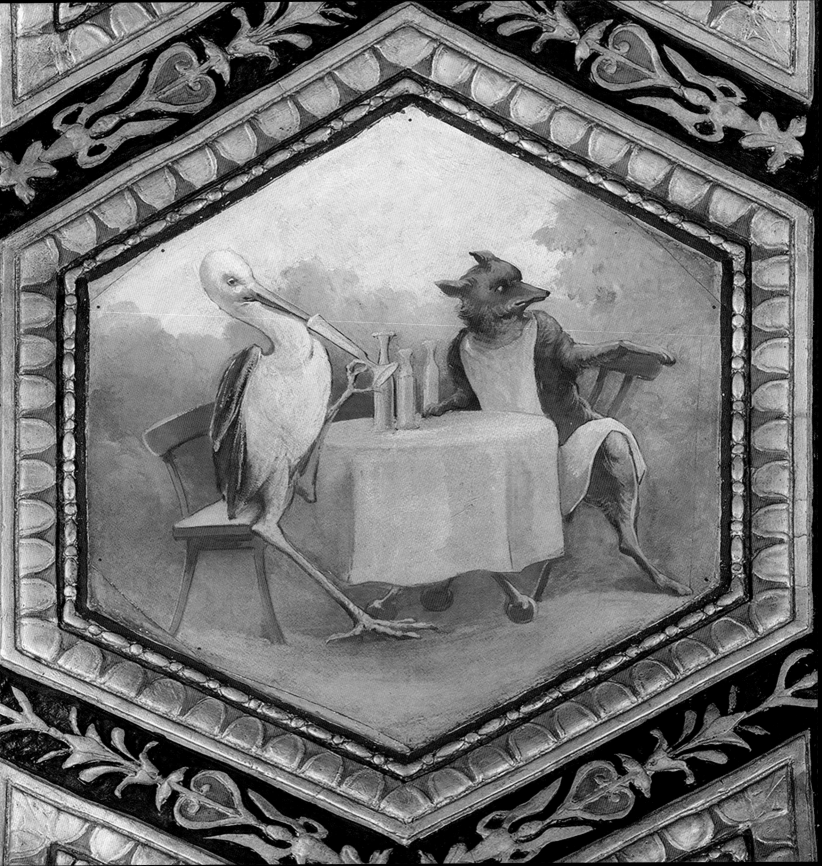

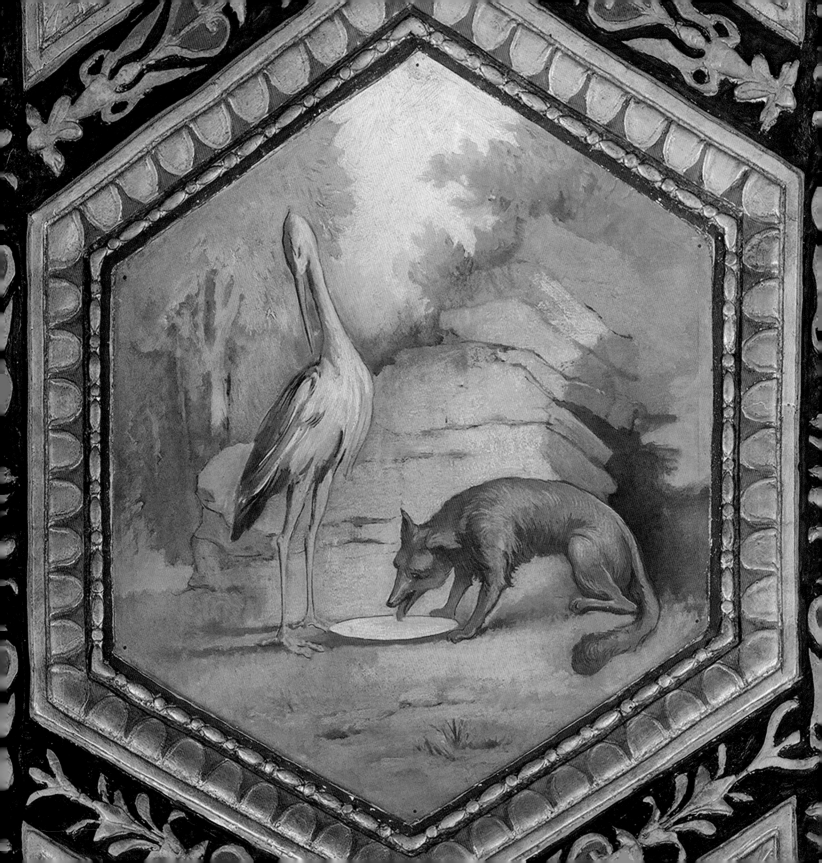

FINE ARTS ROOM

EMMA CIARDI (1879–1933)

Emma Ciardi was born in Venice. Her father, Guglielmo, and brother Beppe were also painters, allowing Ciardi to begin painting as an adolescent. She exhibited for the first time at the Exposition Universelle in Paris in 1900 and later at the Promotrice in Turin at the Esposizione. She soon made a name for herself with her impressionism painting, which was well received by the English and American public. In 1910 she organized her first solo exhibition at the Leicester Galleries in London, followed by a second in 1913. Additional exhibitions followed at London's Fine Art Society in 1928 and 1933. In the United States she exhibited at the Howard Young Gallery in New York, which obtained exclusive rights to sell her work.

WORKS:
Serene Morning
Al Fresco
Dances & Madrigals
Under the Trees
A Short Rest

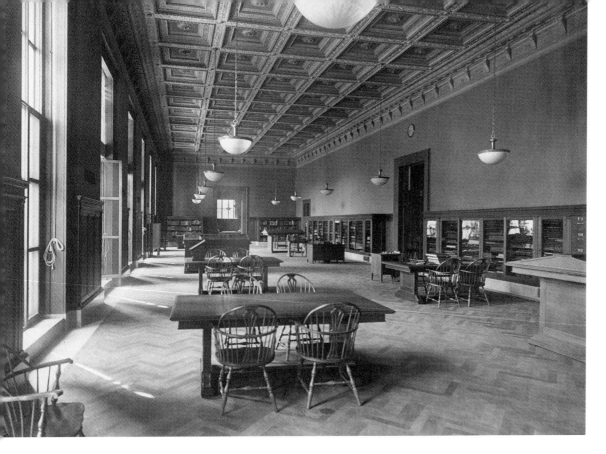

Undated photo of reading room known as the Fine Arts Room. Note door windows to the loggia are open. The coffered ceiling was copied from the Church of Santa Maria Maggiore, Rome. *Photograph courtesy of the Burton Historical Collection, Detroit Public Library.*

RIGHT: *Serene Morning* by Emma Ciardi. Gift from William A. Fisher, 1956. *Photograph courtesy of Martin Vecchio.*

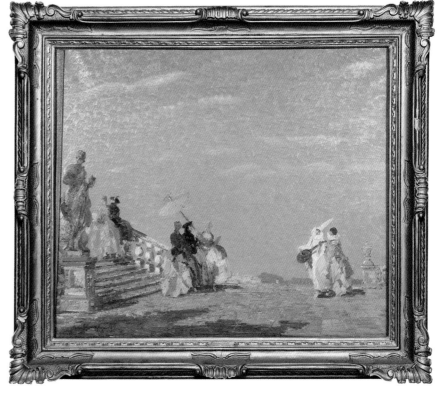

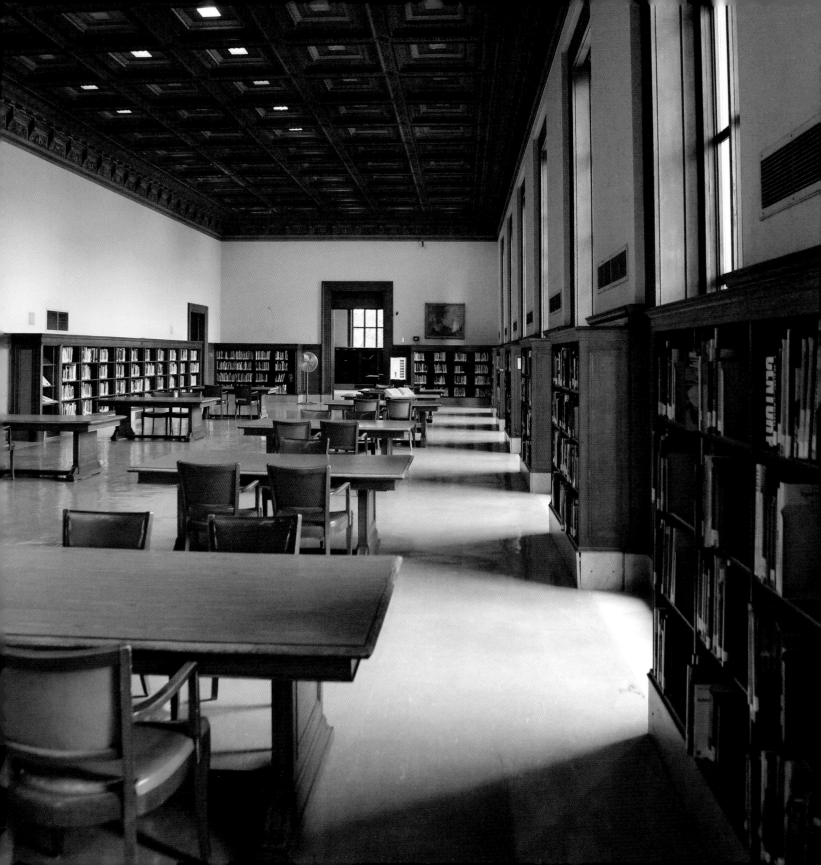

FACING PAGE: The Fine Arts Room today. *Photograph ©
Jeffrey A. Scherer, FAIA.*

_____

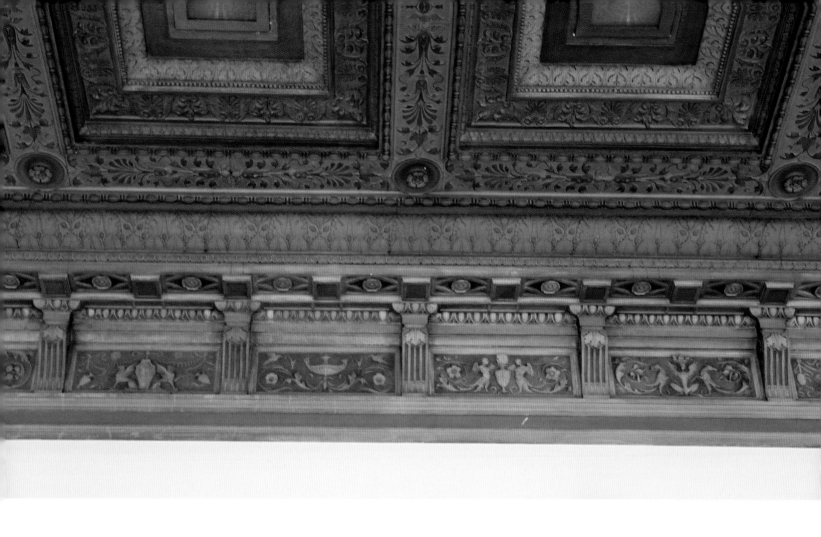

FACING PAGE: The frieze is separated into panels by pairs of brackets equally spaced about the room. The ceiling hues are blue and gold. Geometric shapes of squares and circles are surrounded by rosettes and acanthus leaves. *Photograph © Jeffrey A. Scherer, FAIA.*

FACING PAGE: The Yellin Gate welcomes visitors to the Fine Arts Room. *Photograph courtesy of the Burton Historical Collection, Detroit Public Library.*

THE METAL WORKER: SAMUEL YELLIN (1885–1940)

Samuel Yellin was one of the twentieth century's foremost artisans in iron and an extraordinary educator and businessman. Born in 1885 in Mogilera, Poland, he was recognized at an early age for his drawing ability and interest in iron work. He received an apprenticeship with a local Russian blacksmith and by age sixteen became a mastersmith. In 1906 he immigrated to America and resided in Philadelphia, where he enrolled in classes at the Philadelphia Museum of Industrial Art. Because of his skill level, within one year he was asked to teach iron-work classes.

In 1909 he opened Samuel Yellin Metalworkers, which has been in continuous operation ever since. During the building boom of the 1920s, Yellin's studio employed as many as 250 craftsmen. His work set the standard in quality and design for custom forged metalwork. Today, Yellin Metalworkers operates under the direction of Clare Yellin, granddaughter of Samuel and daughter of Harvey Z. Yellin.

Yellin liked to call himself a metalworker, but others called him a genius. His wrought-iron craftsmanship can be found on some of the finest buildings in America, including the Federal Reserve Bank of New York, the Washington National Cathedral, the Art Institute of Chicago, and Oberlin College in Ohio. His works were installed in numerous buildings and residences in the Detroit area including the Detroit Institute of Art, the University of Michigan Law School, the Cathedral of the Most Blessed Sacrament, the Edsel Ford home in Grosse Pointe, Michigan, and the Detroit residences of Benjamin Siegal and John Newberry.

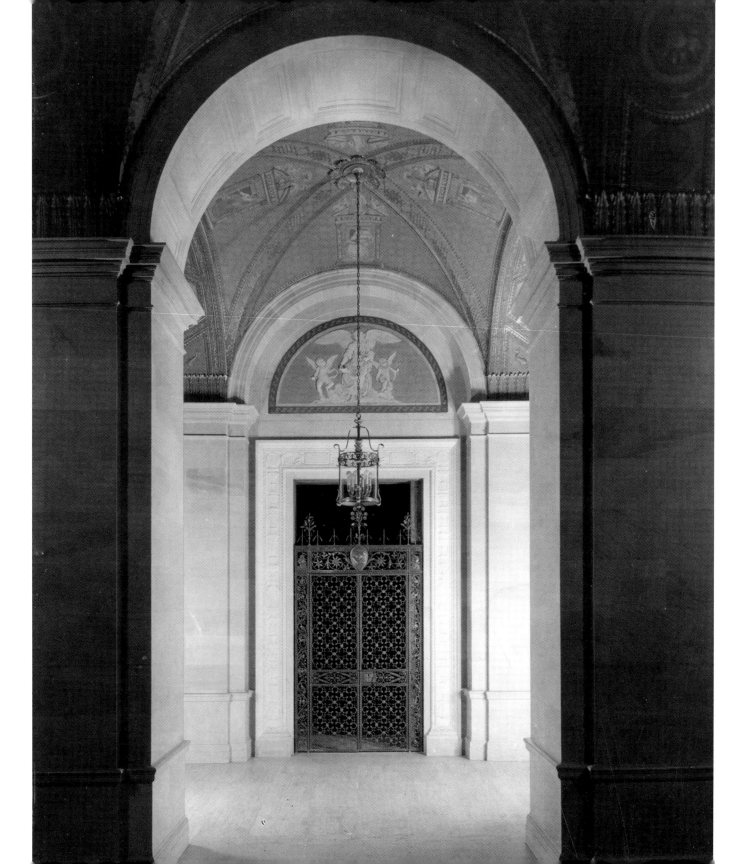

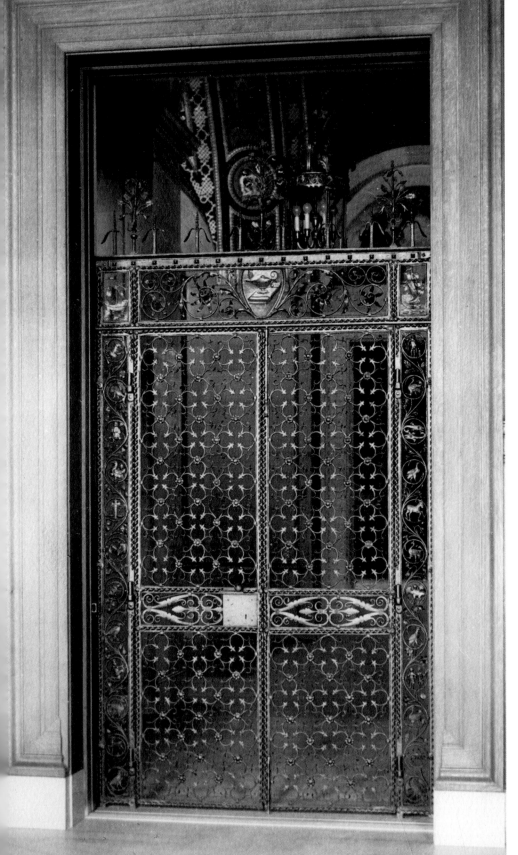

The Yellin Gate. Note the lamp with book at the top of the gate and signs of the zodiac adorning the vertical side panels. *Photograph courtesy of the Burton Historical Collection Detroit Public Library.*

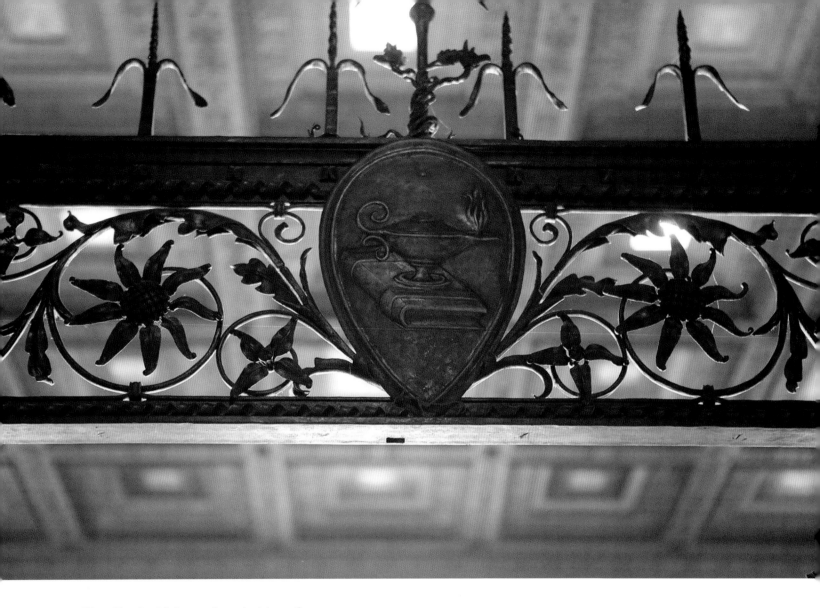

Closed book with lamp adorned with sunflowers.
Photograph © Jeffrey A. Scherer, FAIA.

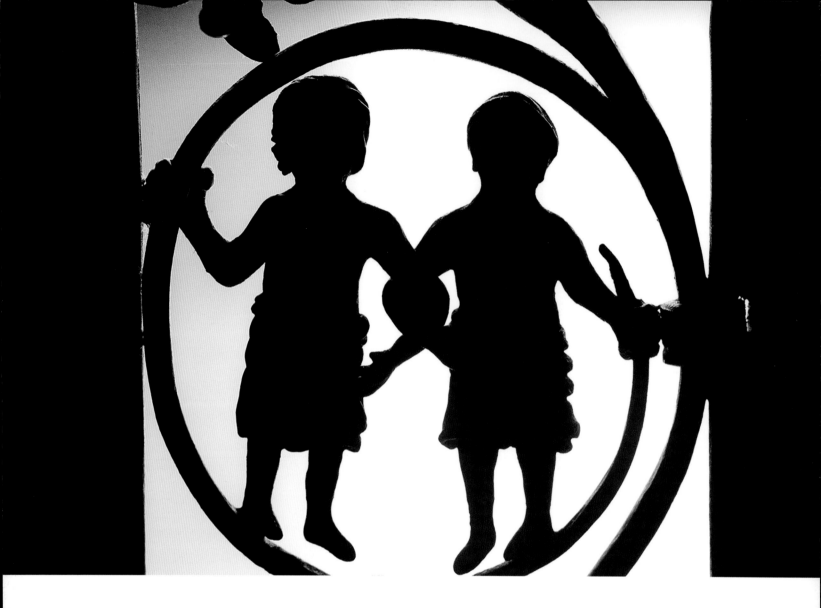

ABOVE: Yellin Gate detail of Gemini, the twins. *Photograph courtesy of Trista Dymond.*

OPPOSITE: Yellin Gate featuring quatrefoil design and rosettes. *Photograph courtesy of Trista Dymond.*

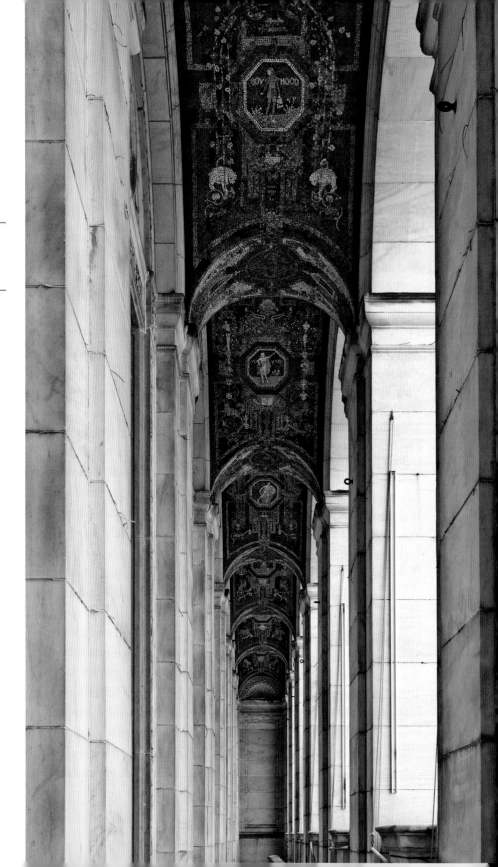

The loggia today. *Photograph courtesy of Martin Vecchio.*

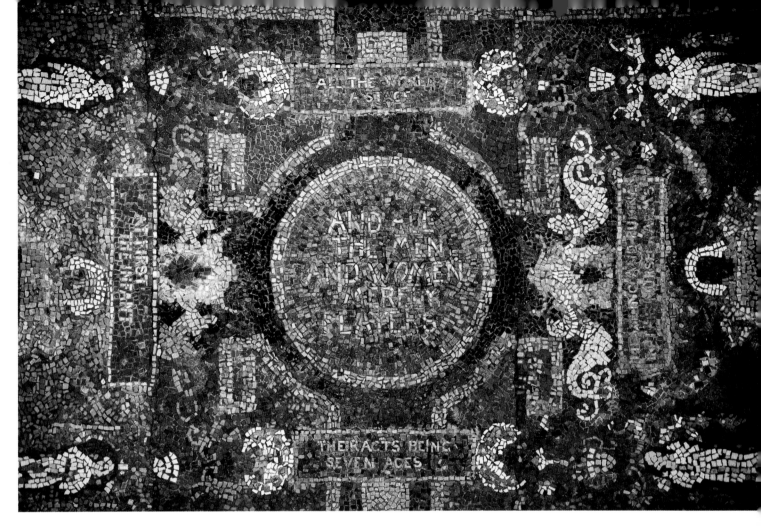

The first arch represents Infancy, the first age of man. Inside the circle reads: "And all the men and women merely players." *Photograph courtesy of Timothy Griffin.*

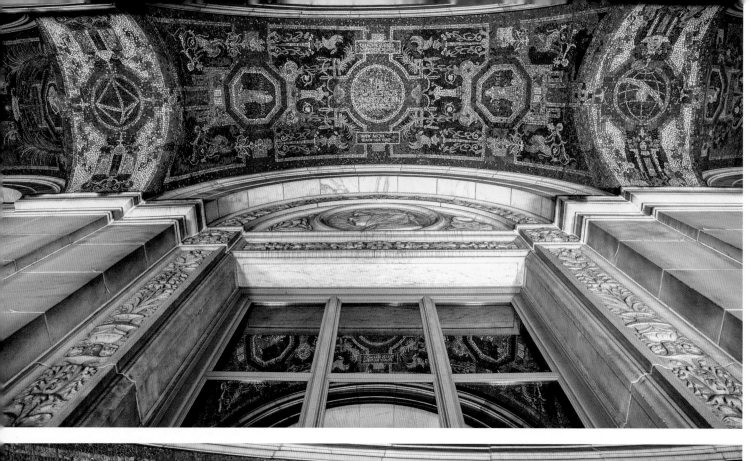

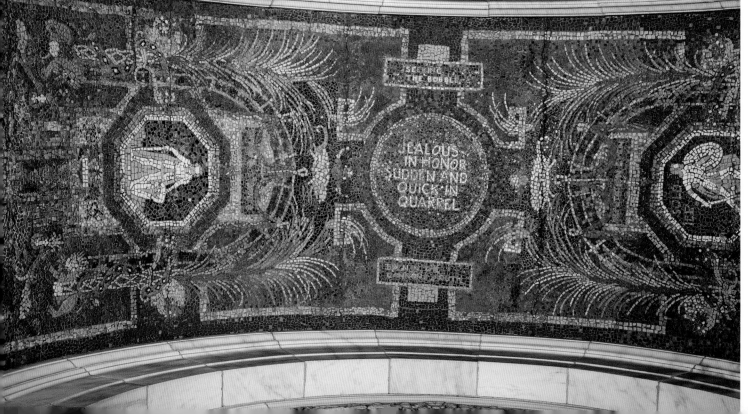

JEALOUS
IN HONOR
SUDDEN AND
QUICK IN
QUARREL

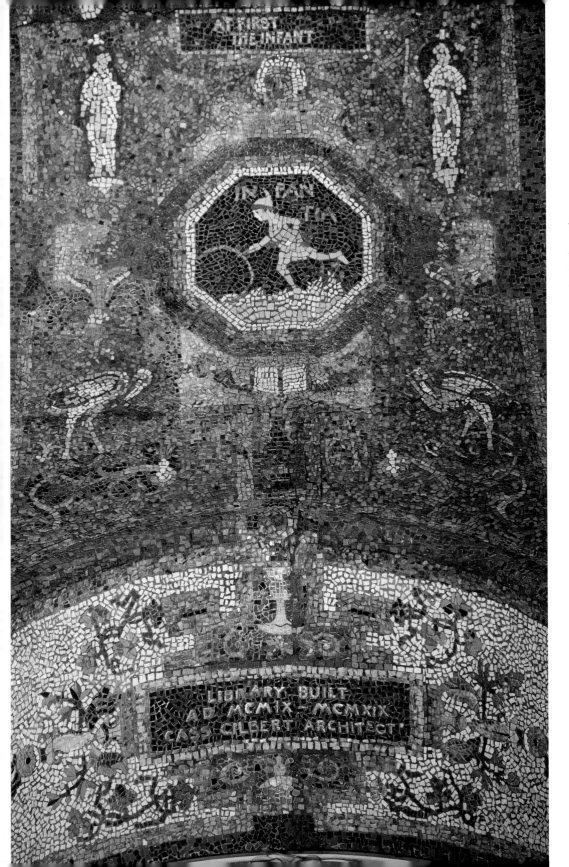

Architect Cass Gilbert's "signature" installed on the ceiling of the south end of the loggia reads:

LIBRARY BUILT

A.D. MCMIX — MCMXIX

CASS GILBERT ARCHITECT

Photograph courtesy of Joy VanBuhler.

FACING PAGE: The fourth age of man is Soldier. In tile are the words "Jealous in honor sudden and quick in quarrel." The fifth age of man is Justice. Writing in tile: "Full of wise saws and modern instances." *Photographs courtesy of Joy VanBuhler.*

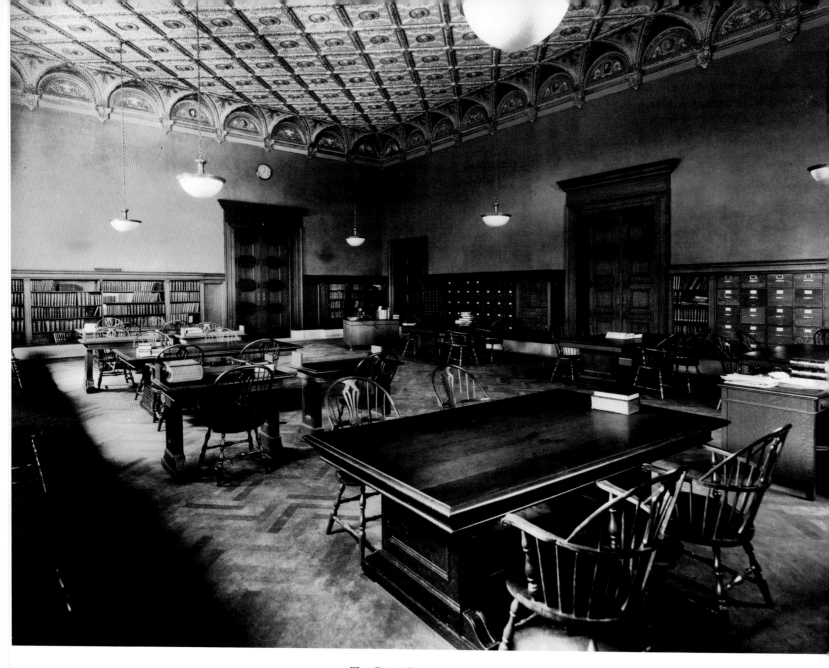

The Civics Room upon completion. The ceiling is a replica of the Doge's Palace, Venice, and features extravagant use of pendentives, corbels, and lunettes. *Photograph courtesy of the Burton Historical Collection, Detroit Public Library.*

Books are the most enduring monuments of man's achievements.
Through them civilazation becomes cumulative.

<small>CASS GILBERT</small>

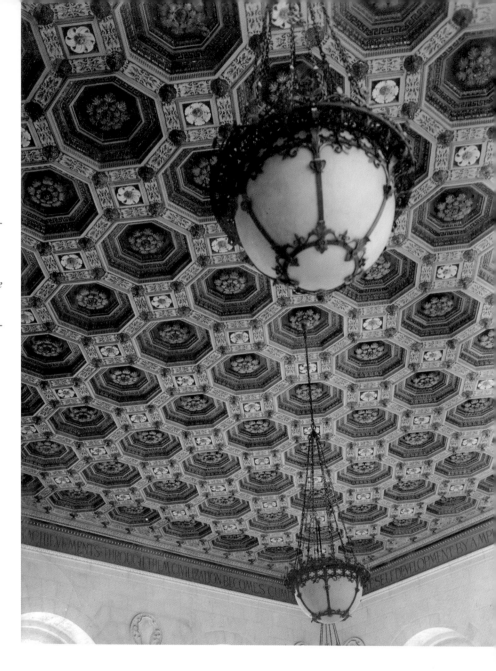

Designed by Wiley, the ceiling is a geometrical arrangement of rosettes and caissons painted in red, blue, violet, and gold. *Photograph courtesy of the Burton Historical Collection, Detroit Public Library.*

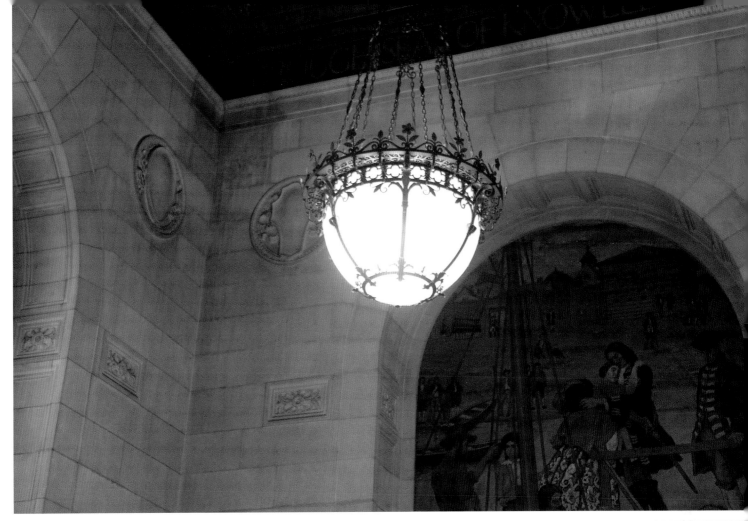

ABOVE: Five chandeliers cast by Sterling Bronze Company, New York, continue to glow in the Delivery Hall. Two versions of cow's skulls are situated below the cornice, and Gari Melcher's *The Landing of Cadillac's Wife, 1703,* is on the right. *Photograph © Jeffrey A. Scherer, FAIA.*

RIGHT: Rosettes and Greek key design adorn the ceiling. *Photograph courtesy of Timothy Griffin.*

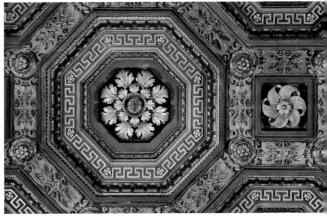

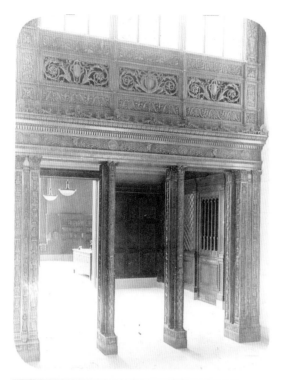

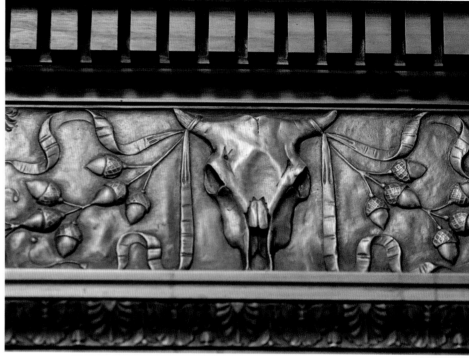

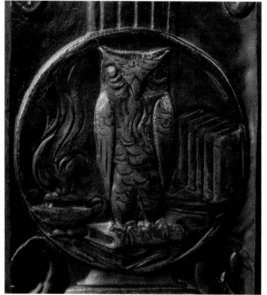

TOP LEFT: Five identical bronze doorways designed by John Donnelly Sr. provide entries into the Delivery Hall. Decorated in low relief, symbolic cow's skulls, books, owls, lamps, and griffins adorn columns with Corinthian capitals. *Photograph courtesy of the Burton Historical Collection, Detroit Public Library.*

TOP RIGHT: The bas-relief of the cow's skull decorated with garlands was a common form of decorating in classical architecture and often used on walls and in temples. Acorns celebrate the growth of the great oak tree. *Photograph courtesy of Trista Dymond.*

LEFT: The owl symbolizes wisdom; the lamp, enlightenment; and the closed book represents knowledge yet to be discovered. *Photograph courtesy of Trista Dymond.*

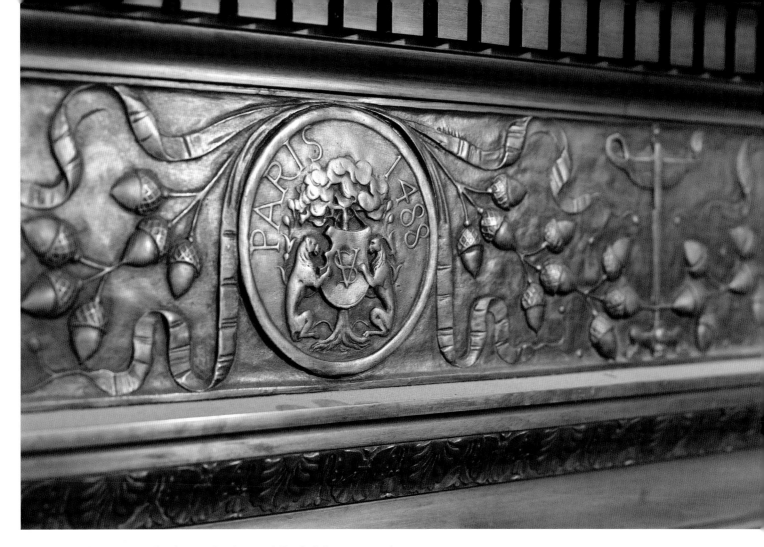

Printer's marks were popular during the Arts and Crafts Movement and were often incorporated as decoration in architecture. The marks are emblems or symbols of trademark used by early printers beginning in the fifteenth century. *Photograph courtesy of Martin Vecchio.*

Thielman Kerver, Paris, 1488
Johann Gruninger, Strasburg, 1483
Foulis Press, Glasgow, 1740
Aldus Manutius, Venice, 1494
Chiswick Press, London, 1811
New York City Coat of Arms, 1733

Book Lover's Room / E. Azalia Hackley Collection

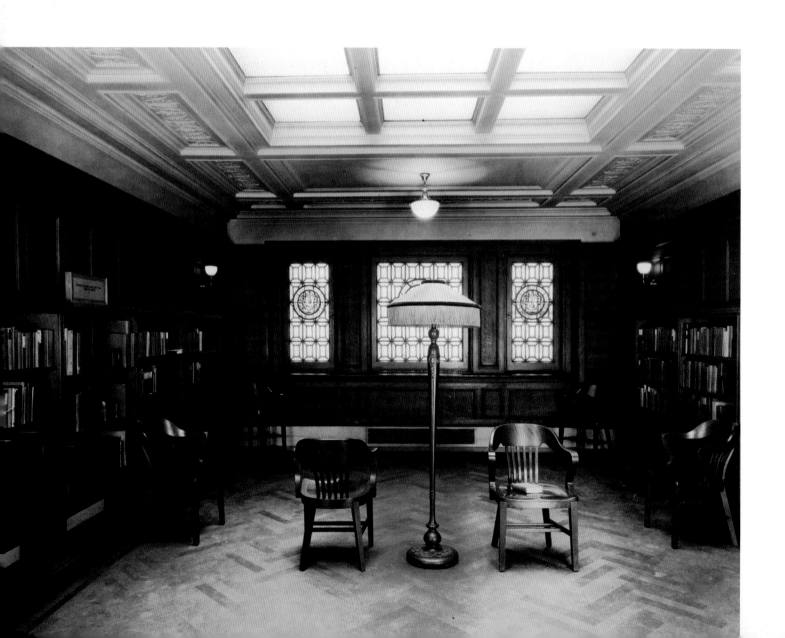

The Book Lover's Room, adjacent to Adam Strohm Hall, is now known as the Reading Room of the E. Azalia Hackley Collection of African Americans in the Performing Arts. *Photograph courtesy of the Burton Historical Collection, Detroit Public Library.*

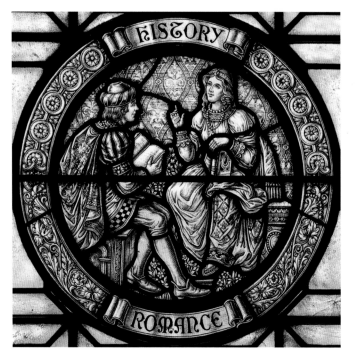

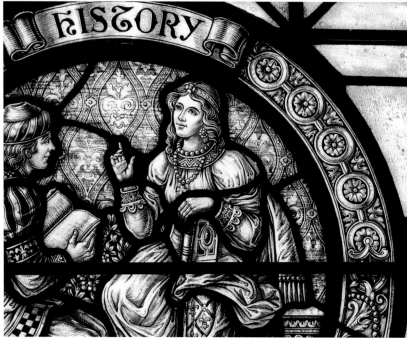

Wiley created three painted windows, which make a delightful backdrop for the Book Lover's Room. In the center is an image of a man and a woman reading; on the left a candle and an ink-well represent ethics and stage; on the right an owl and a book represent cosmos and life. *Photographs courtesy of Trista Dymond.*

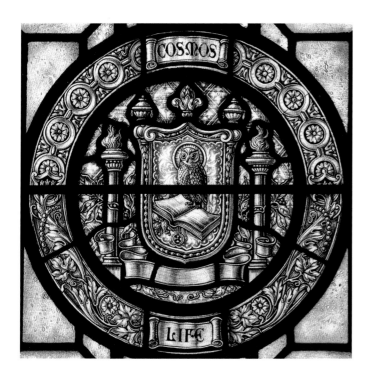

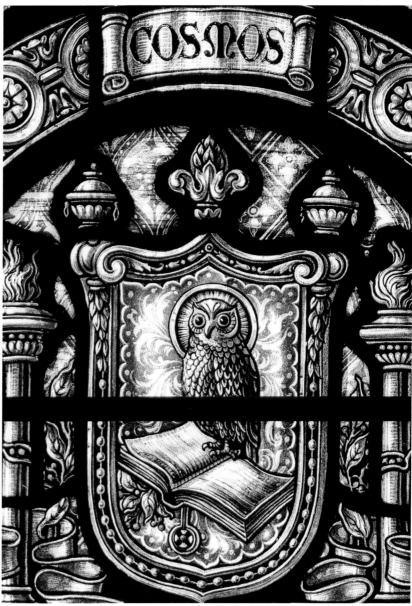

Music Room

The Music Room (formerly known as the Music and Drama Room), features a coffered ceiling adapted from the Ducal Palace, Mantua, Italy. The ceiling features gold and blue rosettes within caissons. *Photograph courtesy of the Burton Historical Collection, Detroit Public Library.*

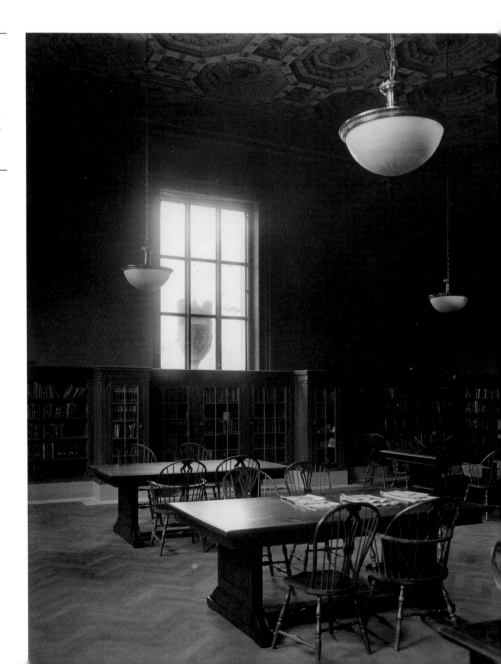

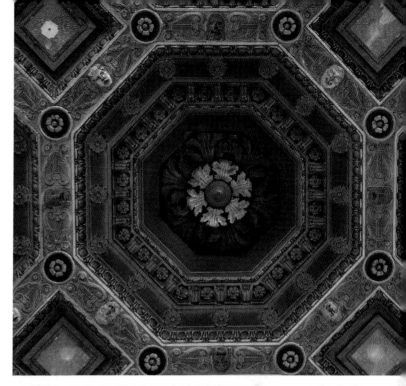

TOP RIGHT: Octagonal frames showcase the details of the ceiling where lyres and masks representing music and drama are placed on bands between the caissons. *Photograph courtesy of John Campbell.*

BOTTOM RIGHT: View of a man wearing headphones listening to a phonographic record from the music collection and following along with a musical score. *Photograph courtesy of the Burton Historical Collection, Detroit Public Library.*

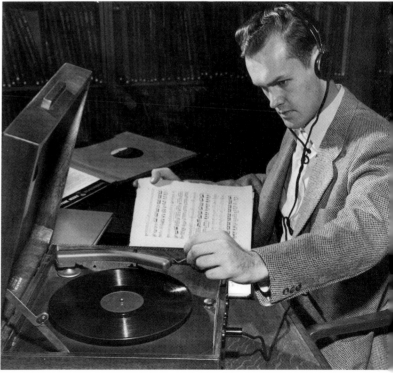

RIGHT: Once a place of live performances, the Music and Drama Room designed by Cass Gilbert features double pocket doors to minimize musical sounds that may have disturbed other library patrons. The floor was composed of pressed cork for further insulation. *Photograph © Jeffrey A. Scherer, FAIA.*

BELOW: Bronze doorplate of pocket doors with letters "DCL" intertwined (Detroit City Library). Note the rosettes on the horizontal panel and a lighted torch at the top of each vertical panel. *Photograph © Jeffrey A. Scherer, FAIA.*

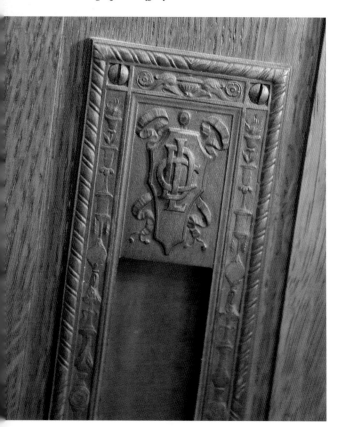

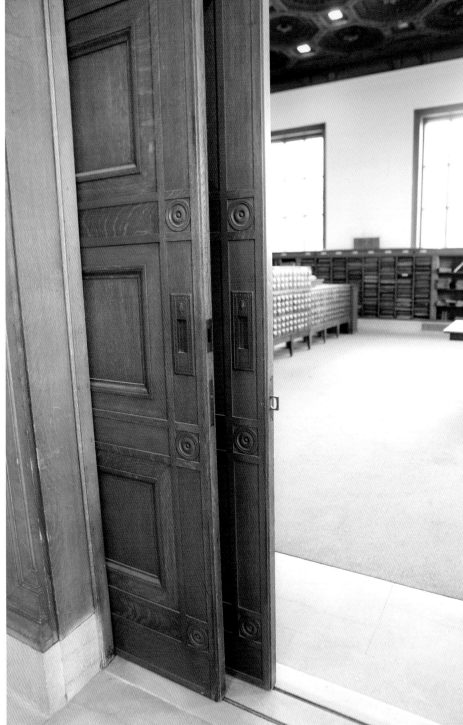

The Detroit Public Library at night, November 15, 1950. Photograph taken from the steps of the Detroit Institute of Art. *Photograph courtesy of the Burton Historical Collection, Detroit Public Library.*

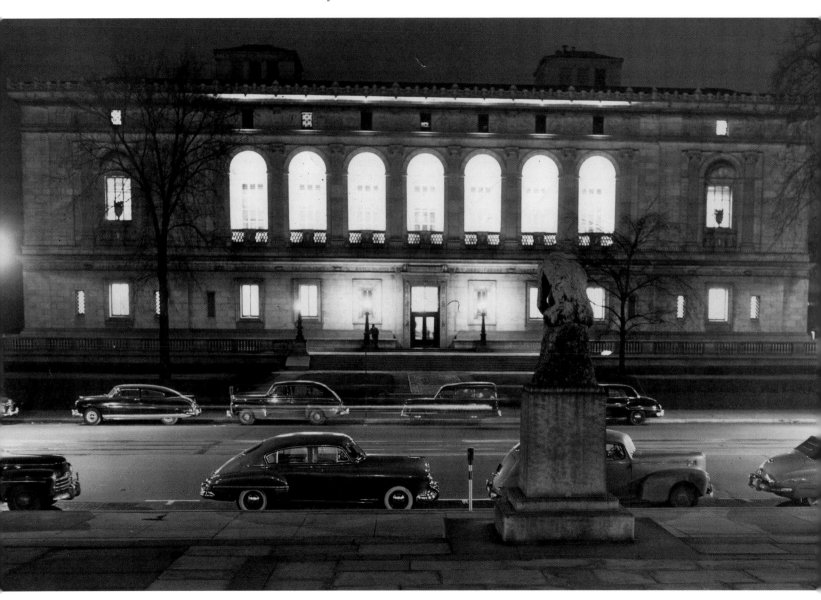

The only thing you absolutely have to know is the location of the library.

ALBERT EINSTEIN

THE 1963 ADDITION

Beginning in 1926, just five years after the new Detroit Public Library opened, discussions were underway regarding building new wings. On December 11, 1926, *Detroit Saturday Night* quoted Adam Strohm, library director: "Some of our departments are, during two thirds of the year, crowded to the point where congestion is serious, where waiting lines are part of the common daily institutional life, where attendants are on the verge of the breaking point in simply carrying out the mechanical processes, with little opportunity left for personal service and the capitalization of professional experience and expert knowledge."

In 1944, Cass Gilbert Jr. and Francis Keally were selected by the Library Commission as architects for the new addition. In 1955, final plans were approved and the Commission worked to resolve issues of bond interest and additional funding requirements.

THE ARCHITECTS: FRANCIS KEALLY (1889–1978)

Born in Pittsburgh, Pennsylvania, Francis Keally graduated from the Carnegie Institute of Technology in 1912 and the University of Pennsylvania, where he received his degree in architecture in 1916. He joined the American Institute of Architects in 1919 and obtained fellowship status in 1947. He worked with Cass Gilbert, Trowbridge and Livingston, and Alfred Morton Githens before establishing the firm of Keally and Patterson in 1945.

Keally remained loyal to his Pittsburgh home, specifically to the Carnegie Institute of Technology, now Carnegie Mellon University.

In 1938 he and Githens designed a campus plan for the institute, and in 1946 Keally and Patterson created a design for a Women's Dormitory Group.

In addition to designing and constructing his own projects, Keally was an avid proponent of preserving valuable and older buildings within their neighborhoods. He served as president of the Municipal Art Society, was a strong advocate to pass the landmarks law in New York City, and served on the boards of several organizations dedicated to historic preservation. Some of his major achievements include the Detroit Public Library expansion, a public library in Berlin, Germany, the Brooklyn Public Library, and the Oregon State Capital in Salem.

He partnered with Cass Gilbert Jr. to design the addition to the Detroit Public Library.

WORKS:

Detroit Public Library addition, 1963
Ebony doors, 1963
Bronze and stainless steel railing, Burton Reading Room and Concourse Balcony
Wrought-iron grille entry, Adam Strohm Hall, 1955

CASS GILBERT JR. (1894–1975)

Son of Cass Gilbert and Julia Finch, Gilbert Jr. studied at Yale College and later attended art school at Columbia University. He was an architect and collaborated with his father on several projects. Upon his father's death in 1934, Cass Gilbert Jr. completed some of the projects his father had started, including the United States Supreme Court Building in Washington, DC, and the Foley Square Courthouse in New York.

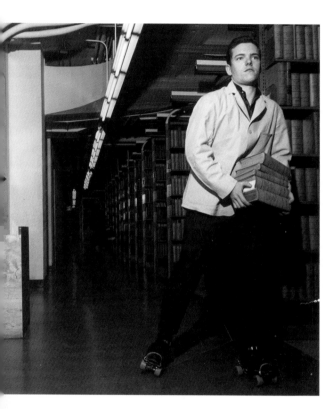

ABOVE: A library page skates through the stacks, 1964. *Photograph courtesy of the Burton Historical Collection, Detroit Public Library.*

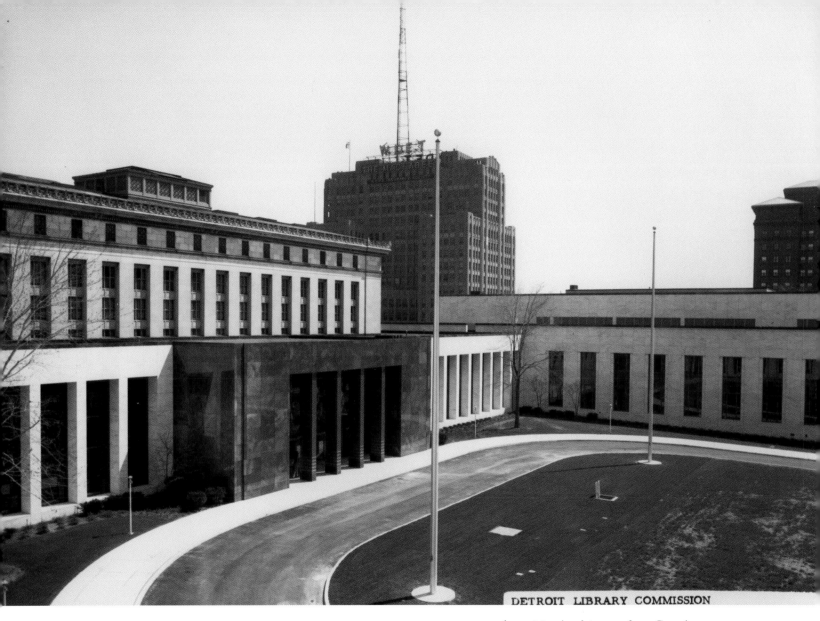

DETROIT LIBRARY COMMISSION

WORKS:

Detroit Public Library addition, 1963

Wrought-iron grille entry, Adam Strohm Hall, 1955

A semicircular driveway from Cass Avenue named for Lewis Cass creates a new library entrance, April 18, 1963. The exterior walls consist of white Vermont marble, Swenson green Maine granite, and glass. *Photograph courtesy of the Burton Historical Collection, Detroit Public Library*

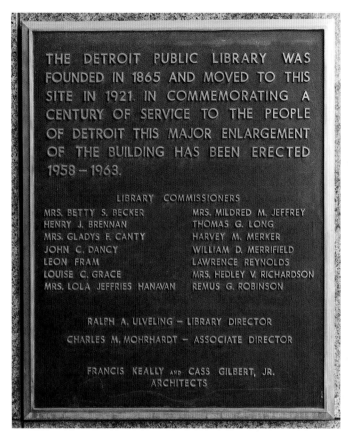

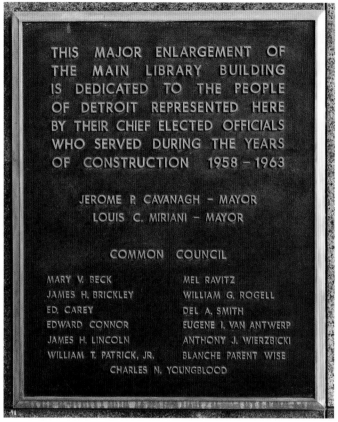

THE DETROIT PUBLIC LIBRARY WAS FOUNDED IN 1865 AND MOVED TO THIS SITE IN 1921. IN COMMEMORATING A CENTURY OF SERVICE TO THE PEOPLE OF DETROIT THIS MAJOR ENLARGEMENT OF THE BUILDING HAS BEEN ERECTED 1958 – 1963.

LIBRARY COMMISSIONERS

MRS. BETTY S. BECKER	MRS. MILDRED M. JEFFREY
HENRY J. BRENNAN	THOMAS G. LONG
MRS. GLADYS F. CANTY	HARVEY M. MERKER
JOHN C. DANCY	WILLIAM D. MERRIFIELD
LEON FRAM	LAWRENCE REYNOLDS
LOUISE C. GRACE	MRS. HEDLEY V. RICHARDSON
MRS. LOLA JEFFRIES HANAVAN	REMUS G. ROBINSON

RALPH A. ULVELING – LIBRARY DIRECTOR

CHARLES M. MOHRHARDT – ASSOCIATE DIRECTOR

FRANCIS KEALLY AND CASS GILBERT, JR.
ARCHITECTS

THIS MAJOR ENLARGEMENT OF THE MAIN LIBRARY BUILDING IS DEDICATED TO THE PEOPLE OF DETROIT REPRESENTED HERE BY THEIR CHIEF ELECTED OFFICIALS WHO SERVED DURING THE YEARS OF CONSTRUCTION 1958 – 1963

JEROME P. CAVANAGH – MAYOR

LOUIS C. MIRIANI – MAYOR

COMMON COUNCIL

MARY V. BECK	MEL RAVITZ
JAMES H. BRICKLEY	WILLIAM G. ROGELL
ED. CAREY	DEL A. SMITH
EDWARD CONNOR	EUGENE I. VAN ANTWERP
JAMES H. LINCOLN	ANTHONY J. WIERZBICKI
WILLIAM T. PATRICK, JR.	BLANCHE PARENT WISE
CHARLES N. YOUNGBLOOD	

Dedication tablets for the 1963 addition, located on the south wall of the Cass Avenue entrance. *Photographs courtesy of Martin Vecchio.*

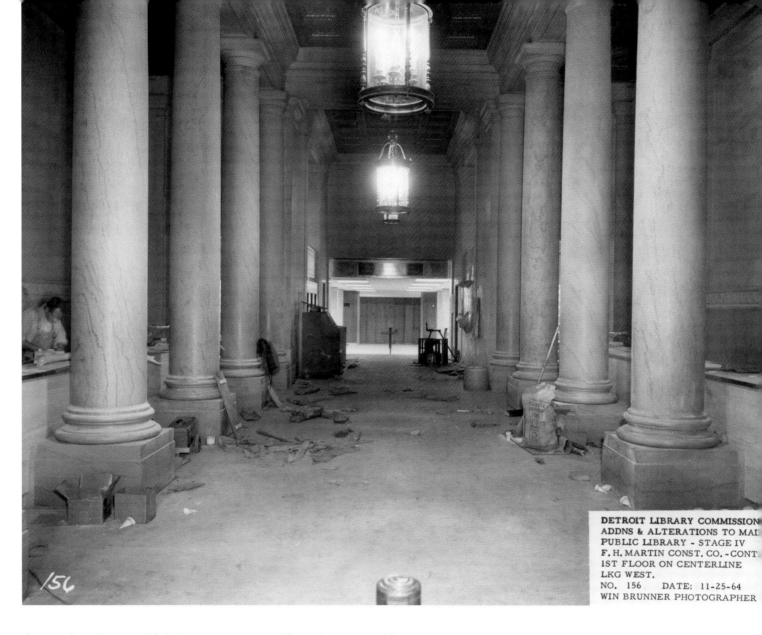

Colonnade in Entrance Hall during construction, November 25, 1964. Note the arched wall has been replaced by an open entry to the Cass Avenue Concourse. *Photograph by Win Bruner, courtesy of the Burton Historical Collection, Detroit Public Library.*

Workers connect the corridor from the Cass Avenue Concourse to the Woodward Avenue Entrance Hall, January 10, 1963. *Photograph by Win Bruner, courtesy of Burton Historical Collection, Detroit Public Library.*

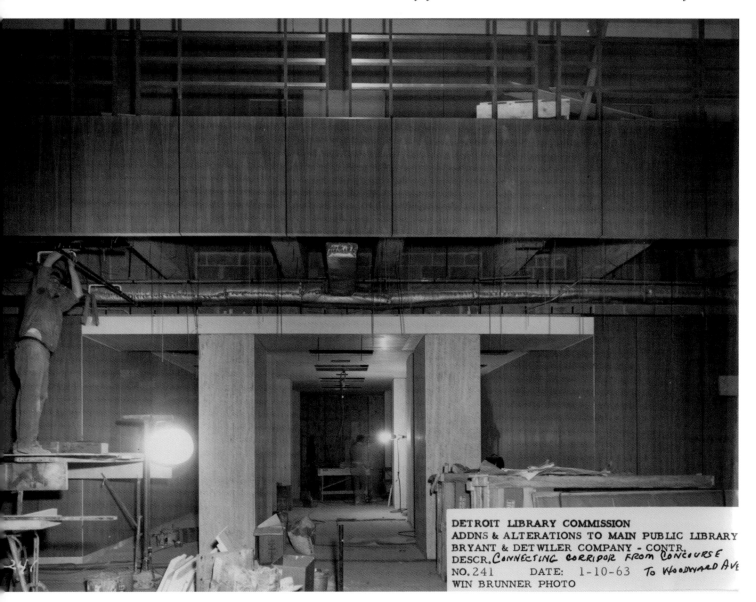

DETROIT LIBRARY COMMISSION
ADDNS & ALTERATIONS TO MAIN PUBLIC LIBRARY
BRYANT & DETWILER COMPANY - CONTR.
DESCR. *Connecting corridor from Concourse*
NO. 241   DATE: 1-10-63 *To Woodward Ave*
WIN BRUNNER PHOTO

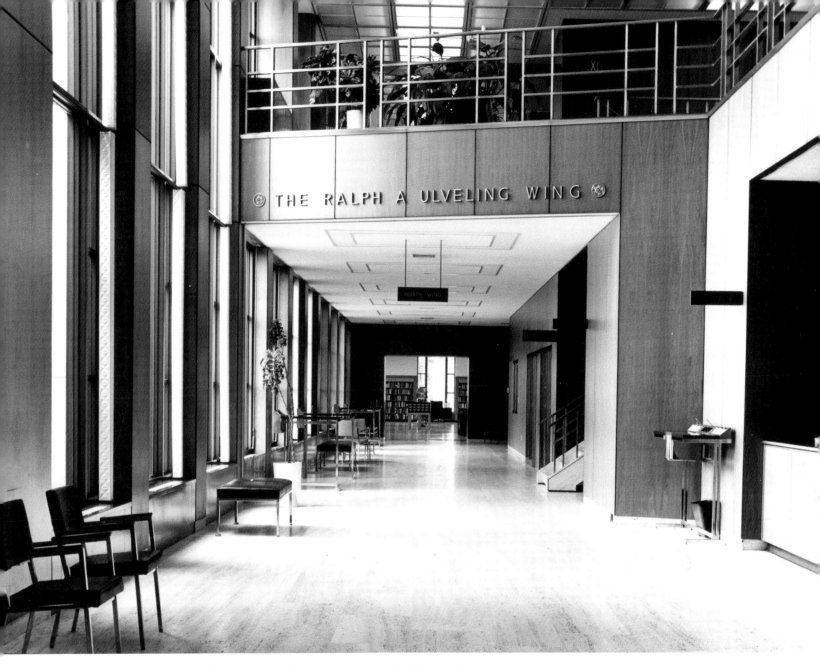

Cass Avenue Concourse looking north. The wing was named in honor of
Ralph A. Ulveling, director of the Detroit Public Library from 1941 to 1967.
Photograph courtesy of the Burton Historical Collection, Detroit Public Library.

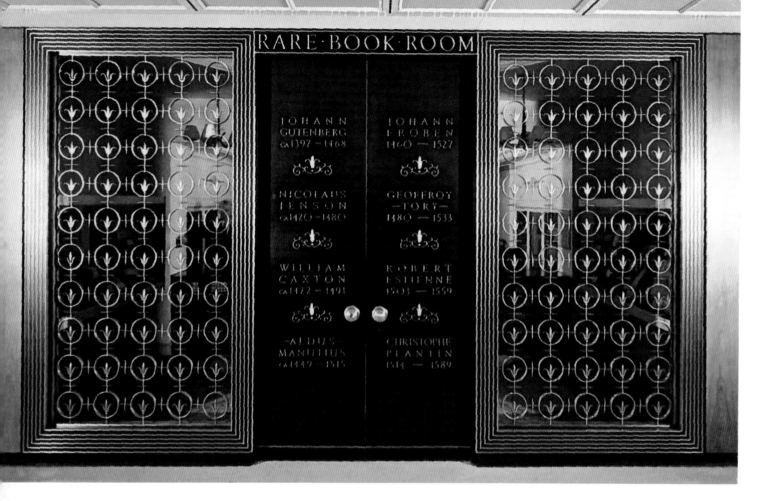

RARE·BOOK·ROOM

JOHANN
GUTENBERG
ca 1397 – 1468

JOHANN
FROBEN
1460 – 1527

NICOLAUS
JENSON
ca 1420 – 1480

GEOFFROY
TORY
1480 – 1533

WILLIAM
CAXTON
ca 1422 – 1491

ROBERT
ESTIENNE
1503 – 1559

ALDUS
MANUTIUS
ca 1449 – 1515

CHRISTOPHE
PLANTIN
1514 – 1589

The Rare Book Room with black ebony doors incised in gold leaf with the names of the most renowned craftsmen in the development of the art of printing. Designed by the architect Francis Keally, the doors are flanked by polished bronze grilles in fleur-de-lis design and suggest the gold tooling of a fine book binding of the sixteenth century based upon the work of Jean Grolier. Given in memory of Dr. Arthur B. McGraw, president of the Friends of the Library, by his widow, Mrs. Leola S. McGraw. *Photographer, Allen Stross postcard published by Center Press.*

FACING PAGE: The completed second-floor concourse. The balcony railing consists of stainless steel and bronze and was designed by the architect Francis Keally. *Photograph courtesy of the Burton Historical Collection, Detroit Public Library.*

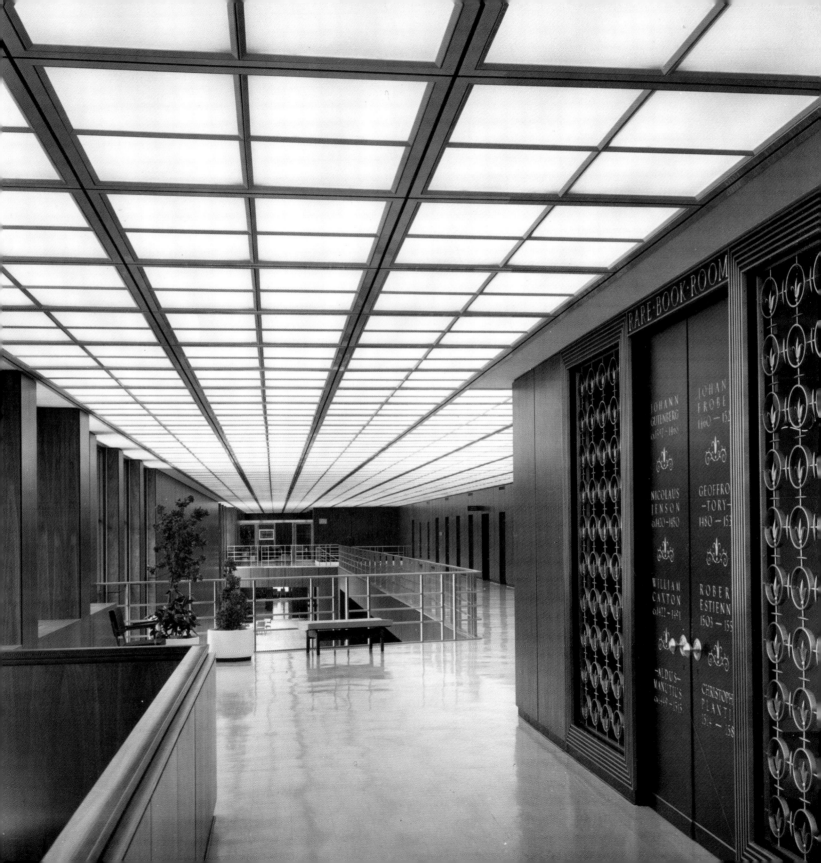

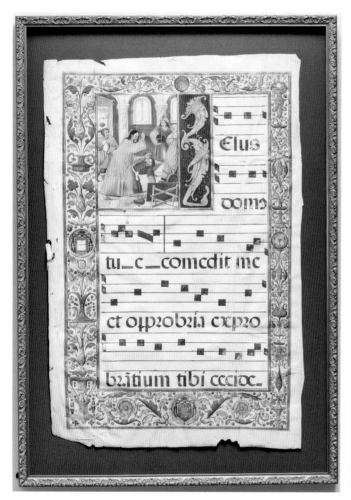
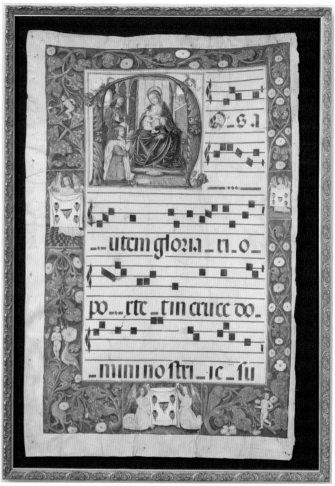

Two fifteenth-century antiphonals decorate the Friends Conference Room, formerly the Rare Book Room. Donated by John S. Newberry to the Friends of the Detroit Public Library. *Photographs courtesy of Martin Vecchio.*

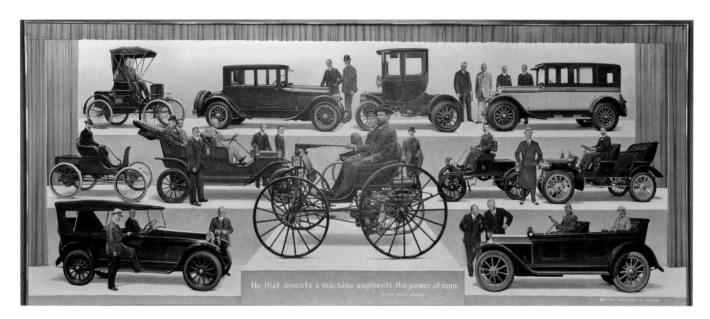

ABOVE: Untitled (History of the American Automobile Industry by Robert Thom, 1976). Commissioned by the Detroit Automobile Dealers Association, the painting was unveiled at the 1976 Detroit Auto Show and later donated to the Detroit Public Library. Twelve automobiles are pictured: 1899 Packard, 1920 Lincoln, 1905 Cadillac, 1924 Chrysler, 1898 Winston, 1908 Model T Ford, 1893 Haynes, 1893 Duryea, 1902 Oldsmobile, 1905 Buick, 1918 Nash, and 1911 Chevrolet. Twenty-seven automobile personalities are portrayed: David Buick, Roy D. Chapin, Louis Chevrolet, Walter Chrysler, James Couzens, John and Horace Dodge, William C. Durant, Charles and Frank Duryea, Edsel and Henry Ford, Norval A. Hawkins, Elwood G. Haynes, Charles F. Kettering, William S. Knudsen, Henry M. and Wilfred C. Leland, Charles W. Nash, Ransom E. Olds, James W. Packard, Alfred P. Sloan Jr., Charles E. Sorenson, C. Harold Wills, John N. Willys, Alexander Winton, and Fred Zeder. *Photograph courtesy of Martin Vecchio.*

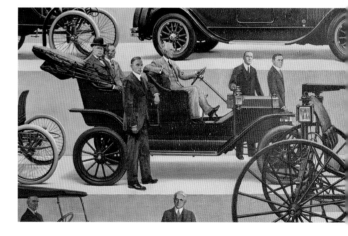

RIGHT: Henry Ford behind the wheel of a 1908 red Model T. Seated in the rear are Edsel Ford and James Couzens. Standing at the rear of the car is C. Harold Wills, the first engineer and designer to work with Henry Ford, and the man in the back far right is Norval Hawkins, the sales genius for the Model T. Leaning on the vehicle at the front is Charles E. Sorenson. *Photograph courtesy of Martin Vecchio.*

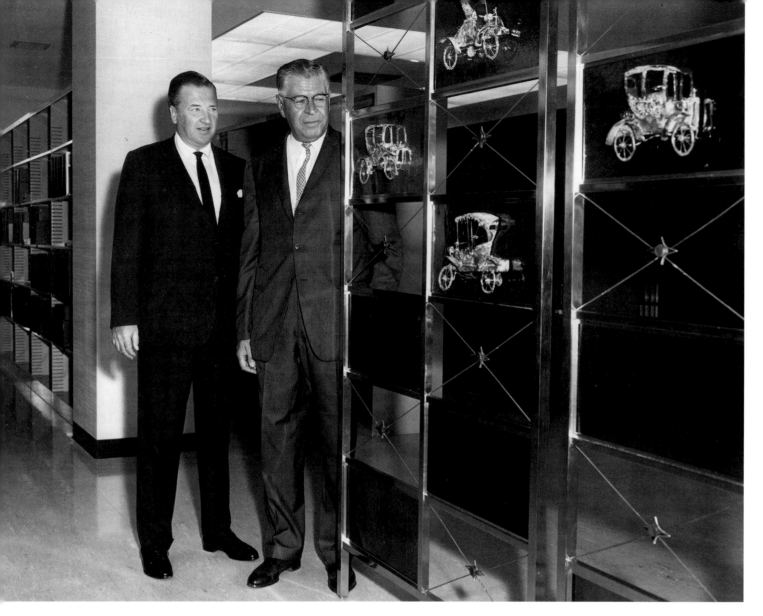

Henry Ford II presents bronze screens to library director Ralph Ulveling as a gift from the Ford Motor Company Fund in 1963. The screens were designed by Malcolm Moran (1923–2011) and Donald Buby (1924–98) of Architectural Sculpture of Birmingham, Michigan. *Photograph courtesy of the Burton Historical Collection, Detroit Public Library.*

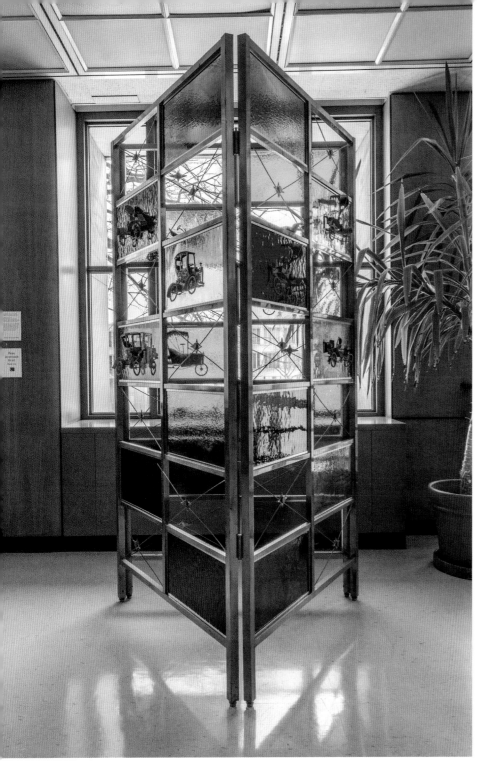

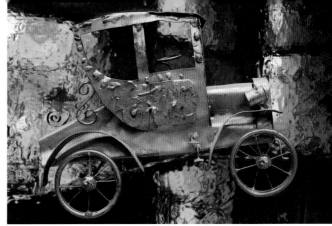

LEFT: One of three hinged, polished bronze screens with cathedral glass insert. Four car designs are featured on glass panels: Ford Model T, Ford Model A, Studebaker Electric, and Buick circa 1908. *Photograph courtesy of Sean Ryan Everett.*

ABOVE: A Studebaker is mounted upon blue cathedral glass. *Photograph courtesy of Kenneth Gabriel.*

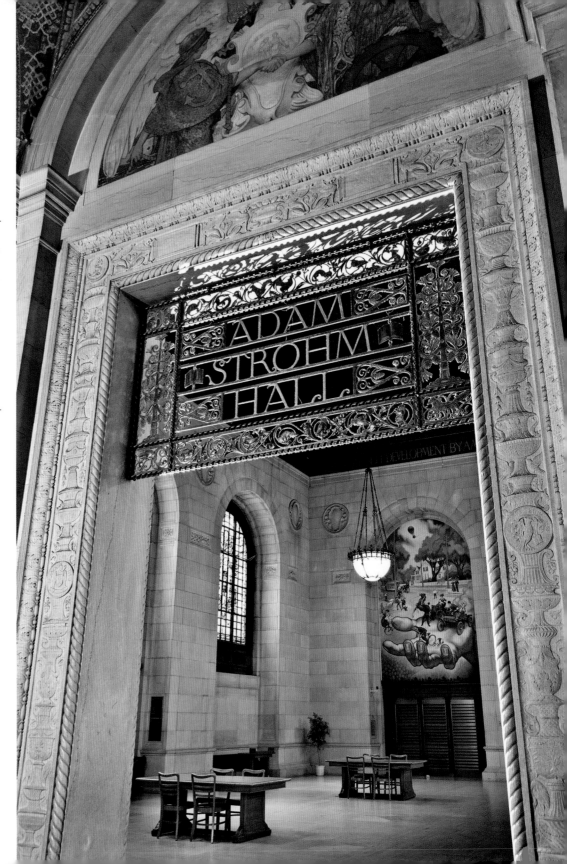

Entrance to the Delivery Hall with grille executed by Harvey Z. Yellin (son of Samuel Yellin), designed by Gertrude Lathrop, Francis Keally, and Cass Gilbert Jr. Donated to the Detroit Public Library by the Detroit Public Library Staff Association in 1955. *Photograph courtesy of Martin Vecchio.*

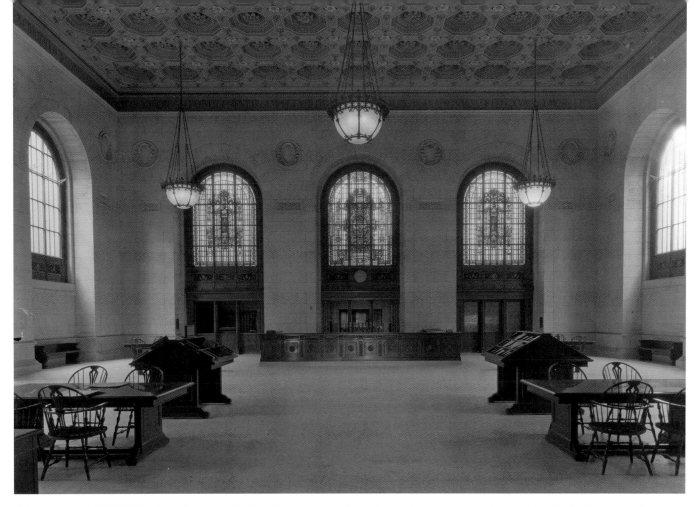

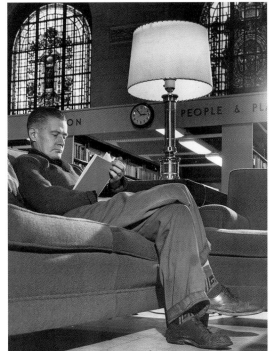

ABOVE: View of the original west windows with hall clock prior to the addition. *Photograph courtesy of the Burton Historical Collection, Detroit Public Library.*

LEFT: Gentlemen reading and relaxing in the Delivery Hall, January 13, 1953. *Photograph courtesy of the Burton Historical Collection, Detroit Public Library.*

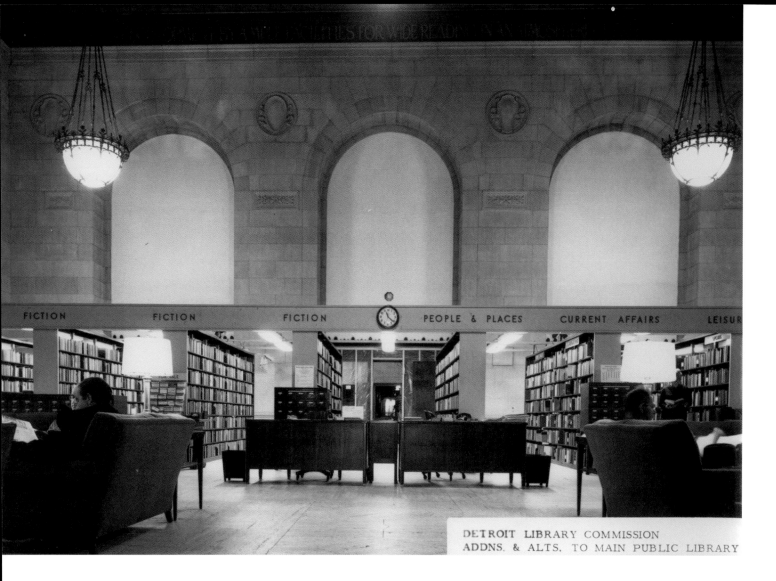

The Delivery Hall, renamed Adam Strohm Hall in honor of Adam Strohm, director of the Detroit Public Library from 1912 to 1941. During construction the painted windows were covered in canvas. Today the windows are no longer visible. *Photograph courtesy of the Burton Historical Collection, Detroit Public Library.*

THE PICTORIALIST:
JOHN STEPHENS COPPIN (1904–1986)

In 1978 John Stephens Coppin was asked, "What do you feel is your greatest accomplishment as an artist?" He replied, "The triptych mural at the Detroit Public Library depicting man's mobility."

Born in Mitchell, Ontario, Coppin knew he wanted to become an artist at a young age. Following a visit to the Toronto Zoo with his grandfather, he was inspired by his grandfather's sketches of the animals. He studied at the Strafford Collegiate Institute and John Wicker Art Academy in Detroit. It was in Detroit that he began his career in art.

Coppin began painting covers for the *Motor News Magazine* (a monthly news magazine for the Automobile Club of Michigan that later became *Michigan Living*) and created over 400 covers. Later he was named the art director for the magazine. Coppin's first studio was located in the Scarab Club Building at 217 Farnsworth in Detroit. He later relocated to Bloomfield Hills, Michigan, where his home became his studio.

Coppin's reputation expanded in Michigan and he was commissioned to do portraits of politicians and industrialists. Some of his noteworthy portraits include Sir Alec Guinness, Henry Ford, William S. Knudsen, Edgar Guest, and Judge Patrick O'Brien, as well as Michigan Governors Murray D. Van Wagoner, Harry S. Kelly, Kim Sigler, and G. Mennen Williams.

Throughout his career Coppin earned several awards including first place at the Michigan Artists Show in 1930, the Scarab Club Gold Medal, and the Hartwig Prize from the Detroit Institute of Arts exhibition in 1953. Coppin retired in 1969 and relocated to Sarasota, Florida, with his wife.

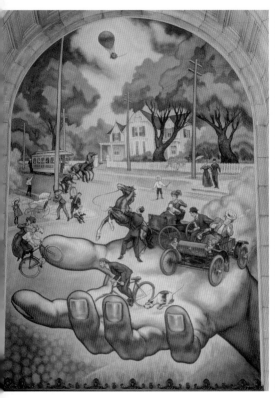 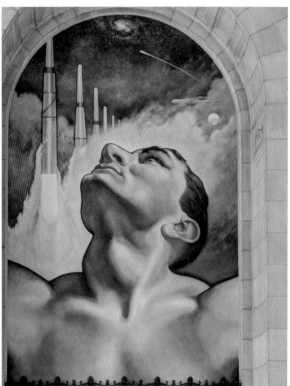 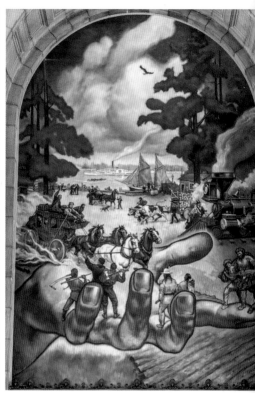

Man's Mobility 1905-1965-1855 (3), oil on canvas, 1963. A triptych mural presents a powerful homage to the progression of transportation. The outstretched hands hold in their palms the past eras as depicted in modes of transportation. Donated to the Detroit Public Library by the Friends of the Detroit Public Library on the occasion of the library system's 100th anniversary in 1965. *Photographs courtesy of William N. Lawrence Jr.*

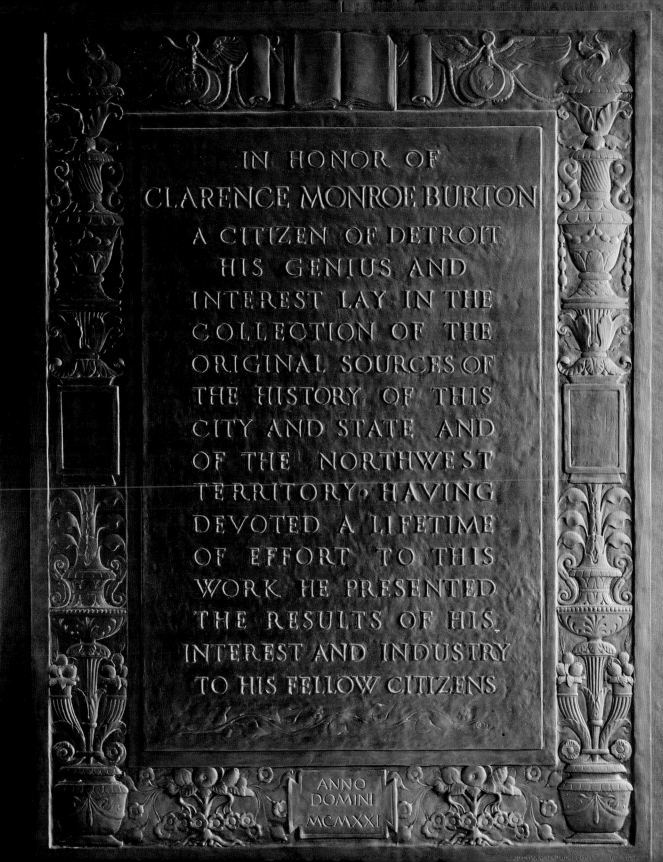

IN HONOR OF
CLARENCE MONROE BURTON
A CITIZEN OF DETROIT
HIS GENIUS AND
INTEREST LAY IN THE
COLLECTION OF THE
ORIGINAL SOURCES OF
THE HISTORY OF THIS
CITY AND STATE AND
OF THE NORTHWEST
TERRITORY · HAVING
DEVOTED A LIFETIME
OF EFFORT TO THIS
WORK HE PRESENTED
THE RESULTS OF HIS
INTEREST AND INDUSTRY
TO HIS FELLOW CITIZENS

ANNO
DOMINI
MCMXXI

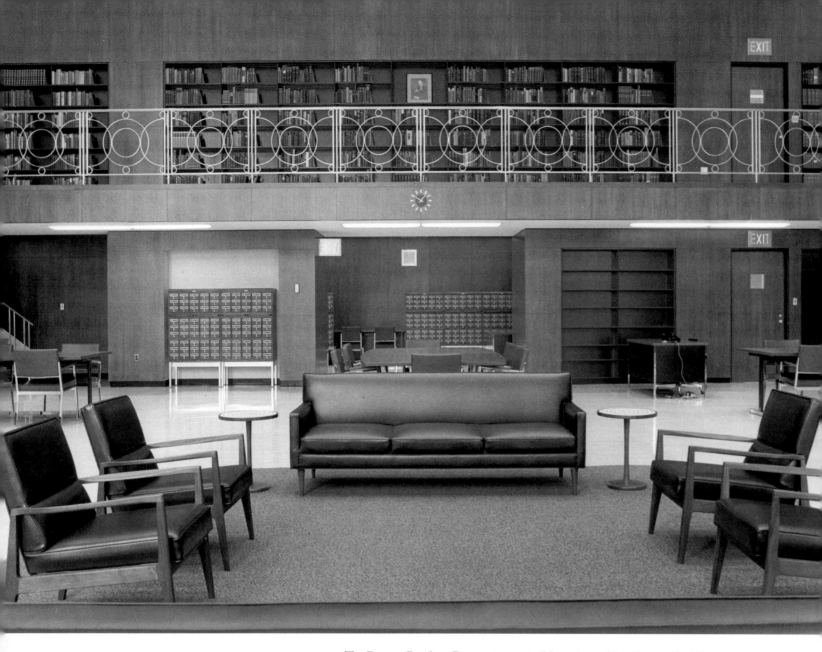

The Burton Reading Room circa 1963. Note the architect's use of mid-century modern design and the repeated use of the stainless steel and brass railing located along the Cass Avenue Concourse. *Photograph courtesy of the Burton Historical Collection, Detroit Public Library.*

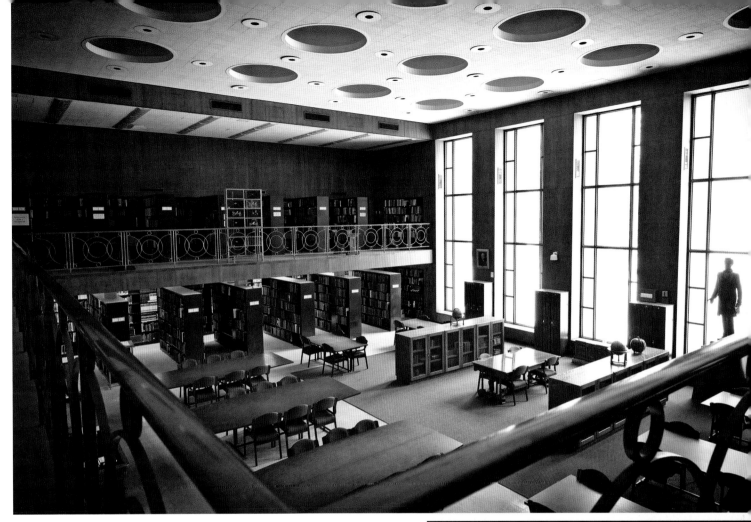

ABOVE: The Burton Reading Room, August 2015. *Photograph courtesy of Martin Vecchio.*

RIGHT: The railing designed by Francis Keally outlines the second-level loft overlooking the Burton Reading Room. *Photograph courtesy of Trista Dymond.*

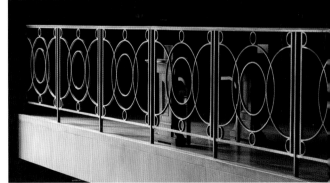

JOHN MIX STANLEY (1814–1872)

John Mix Stanley was an American artist, explorer, and landscape painter known for his Native American portraits and images of tribal life. Born in New York and orphaned at age fourteen, Stanley began painting as a young man. In 1832 he moved to Detroit and earned a living as a house and sign painter. He left Detroit briefly to travel through the Indian Territories and nations, where he acquired his passion for Native American images. In 1864 he returned to Detroit, where he spent the last seven years of his life in his art studio and became involved in the Detroit Museum of Art and its School of Art.

Sadly, over two hundred of Stanley's works were destroyed in two fires in 1865, one at the Smithsonian Institution and the other at the P. T. Barnum American Museum in New York.

Unveiling the Conspiracy, 1862. A depiction of how Major Gladwin had gained knowledge of Pontiac's plans to stage an uprising against the British. The painting shows an Indian girl named Catherine explaining to Major Gladwin why she can no longer come to make moccasins of the elk skins lying in the foreground. *Photograph courtesy of the Burton Historical Collection, Detroit Public Library.*

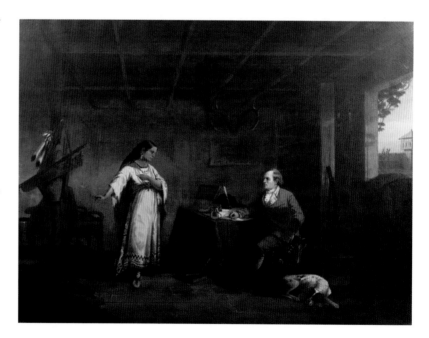

BELOW: Elaborate cabinet of gold and precious metals made by Mariano Alvaraz of Toledo, Spain, in 1883. Commissioned for a member of the Russian royal family, the chest was donated to the Detroit Public Library by Mrs. Charles Sorensen in 1976. *Photograph courtesy of Trista Dymond.*

RIGHT: View of drawers behind cabinet door.
Photograph courtesy of Trista Dymond.

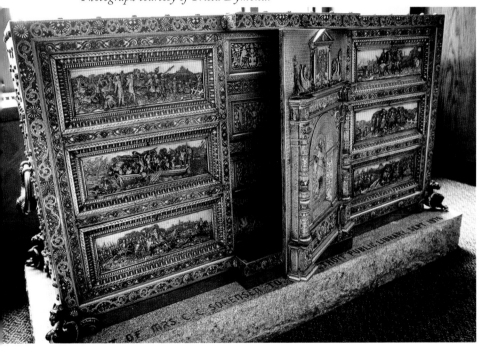

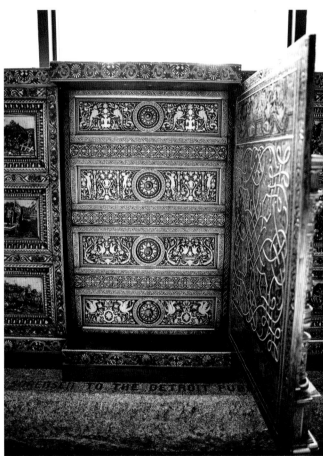

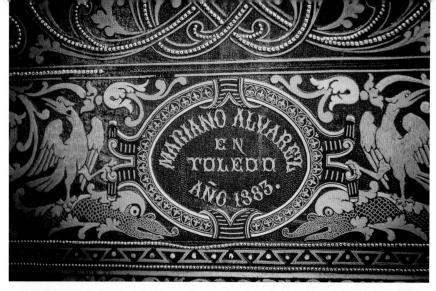

TOP: Artist signature.

MIDDLE: Decorative element of women on drawer.

BOTTOM: Double-headed eagle with coat of arms in bas-relief replicates the city entry gate of Toledo, Spain.
Photographs courtesy of Trista Dymond.

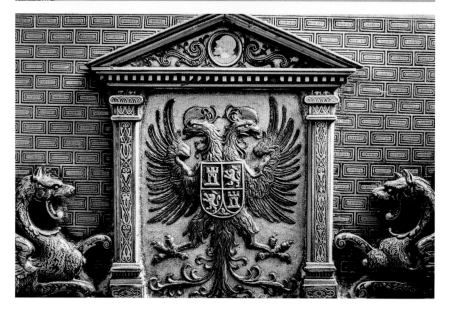

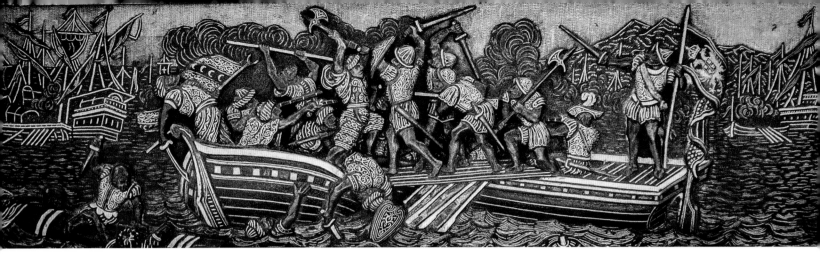

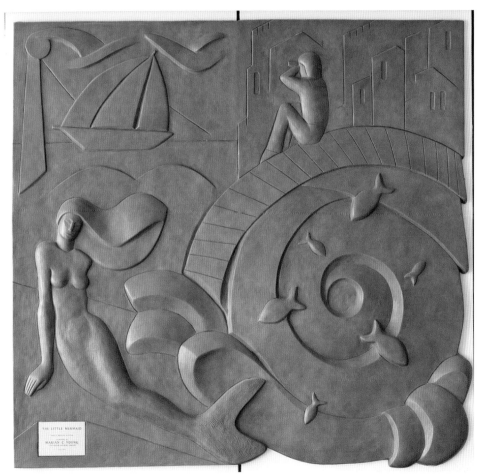

ABOVE: Spanish battle scene in bas-relief on a cabinet drawer. *Photograph courtesy of Trista Dymond.*

LEFT: *The Little Mermaid*, by James C. Young. Given to the Detroit Public Library Children's Room in memory of Marian C. Young, coordinator of children's services. *Photograph courtesy of Martin Vecchio.*

CHARLEY HARPER (1922–2007)

Charley Harper was an American modern artist who developed a unique style integrating simple geometric shapes, color combinations, patterns, and textures. As a child in West Virginia, he was a student of nature, observing and sketching birds. Harper continued to develop his style, which he called "minimal realism," while attending the Art Academy of Cincinnati and later at the Arts Students League in New York.

Harper's illustrations and work have been presented in publications of the National Park Service and the Audubon Society, as well as travel guides published by the Ford Motor Company's *Ford Times.* The holdings of the Detroit Public Library Art Collection include sixteen of Harper's bird images. Two prints were purchased from the artist and fourteen prints were a gift from the Detroit Public Library staff and the Friends of the Detroit Public Library in honor of Agnes Lally, librarian.

SERIGRAPHS, 1963
Horned Grebe
Black-Billed Magpie
Passenger Pigeon
Indigo Bunting
Wood Thrush
Green Jay
Wood Duck
Great Auk
Eskimo Curlew
Rose-Breasted Grosbeak
Carolina Paroquet
Common Murre
Common Warbler
Heath Hen
Red-Eyed Vireo
Western Tanager

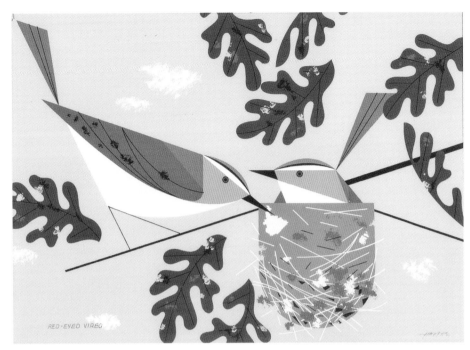

RED-EYED VIREO

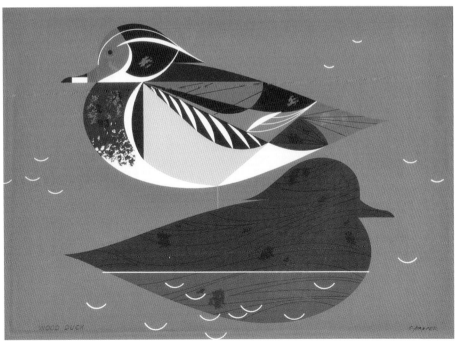

WOOD DUCK

Red-Eyed Virero (top) and *Wood Duck (bottom). Photographs courtesy of Martin Vecchio.*

THE CASS AVENUE ENTRANCE

THE CALIFORNIAN: MILLARD SHEETS (1907–1989)

Millard Sheets was one of the founding members of the "California Scene Painters," artists who created a lasting influence upon generations of western painters. He and a small group worked in California during the 1930s and 1940s and developed a style of watercolor painting that later gave rise to what became known as the California Regionalist school.

Born in Pomona, California, Sheets studied at the Chouinard Art Institute in Los Angeles, graduating in 1929. In 1932 Sheets returned to school to study art and humanities at Scripps College in Claremont, California. Between 1935 and 1941, he began to receive artistic recognition and awards, and his output of high-quality watercolors, oils, and acrylics increased. During World War II, he was an artist-correspondent for *Life Magazine* and the United States Air Force in India and Burma.

In 1953 Sheets founded the Millard Sheets Design Company. The working staff included engineers, architects, draftsmen, and artists for projects which included murals, mosaics, stained glass, and sculpture for private homes and businesses. Sheets designed and completed mural and mosaic work for numerous public buildings in the Los Angeles area and across the nation. Many of the murals and mosaics were for buildings designed by his firm while others were done as independent commissions.

In 1968 Sheets first proposed the murals he designed for Los Angeles City Hall. His design was approved and he was awarded a commission to complete *The Family of Man* murals over the two main

Your painting is a measure of your mind.

MILLARD SHEETS

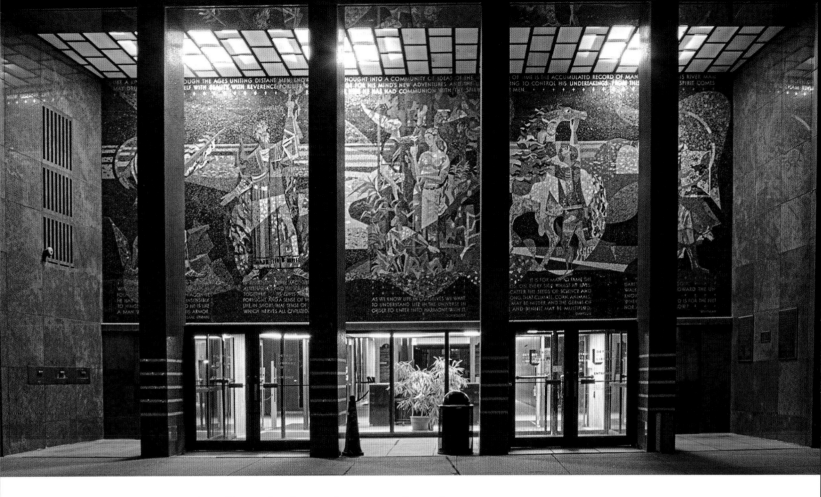

entrances to the building. Sheets also designed mosaics and murals for the Mayo Clinic in Minnesota; the Library at Notre Dame University, South Bend, Indiana; the Scottish Rite Masonic Temple in Los Angeles; several Home Savings and Loan Association buildings in the Los Angeles area; the Detroit Public Library; and the Dome of the National Shrine of the Immaculate Conception in Washington, D.C.

Man's Discovery of His Potential Abilities and His Destiny highlights the newly added Cass Avenue entrance. Consisting of 441,000 pieces of glass, the mosaic's theme is that of individual discovery. Figures include a warrior, a philosopher, a family group, a young man taming a wild stallion, and a navigator holding a chart. The figures are bound together by the symbolic river of knowledge with five glittering inscriptions of gold. Gift from the National Academy of Design's Abbey Fund in 1962. *Photograph courtesy of Kenneth Gabriel.*

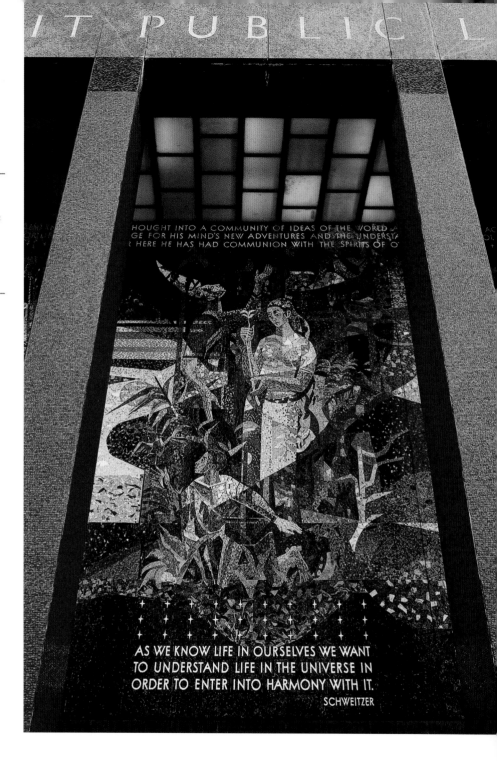

RIGHT: Panel from Millard Sheets mosaic with the following quote by Albert Schweitzer: "As we know life in ourselves we want to understand life in the universe in order to enter into harmony with it." *Photograph courtesy of William Zbaren.*

Floor Plans by Cass Gilbert Jr., and Frances J. Keally, Architects

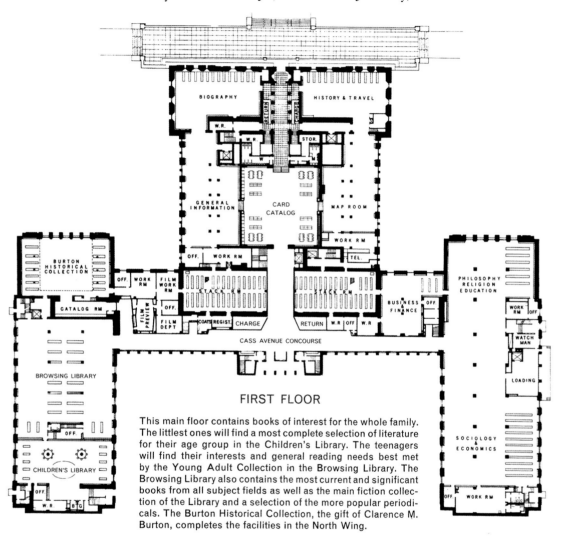

FIRST FLOOR

This main floor contains books of interest for the whole family.
The littlest ones will find a most complete selection of literature
for their age group in the Children's Library. The teenagers
will find their interests and general reading needs best met
by the Young Adult Collection in the Browsing Library. The
Browsing Library also contains the most current and significant
books from all subject fields as well as the main fiction collection of the Library and a selection of the more popular periodicals. The Burton Historical Collection, the gift of Clarence M.
Burton, completes the facilities in the North Wing.

Two areas of special interest along the concourse are the
Educational Film Department, containing an extensive collection of 16mm sound films and filmstrips; and the Business
and Finance Department, containing books, directories, and
periodicals relating to that field of interest. The South Wing
houses the books, magazines, and special materials of the
Sociology and Economics Department and the Philosophy,
Religion, and Education Department.

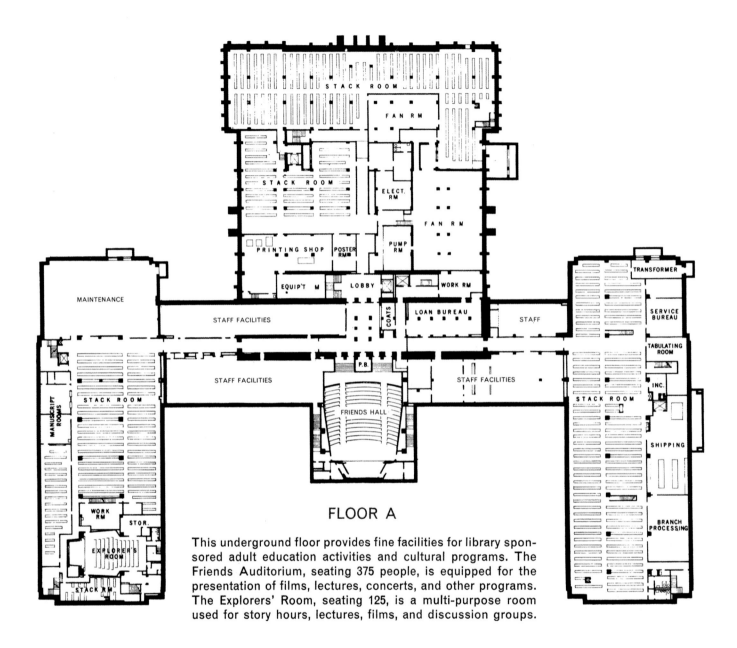

FLOOR A

This underground floor provides fine facilities for library sponsored adult education activities and cultural programs. The Friends Auditorium, seating 375 people, is equipped for the presentation of films, lectures, concerts, and other programs. The Explorers' Room, seating 125, is a multi-purpose room used for story hours, lectures, films, and discussion groups.

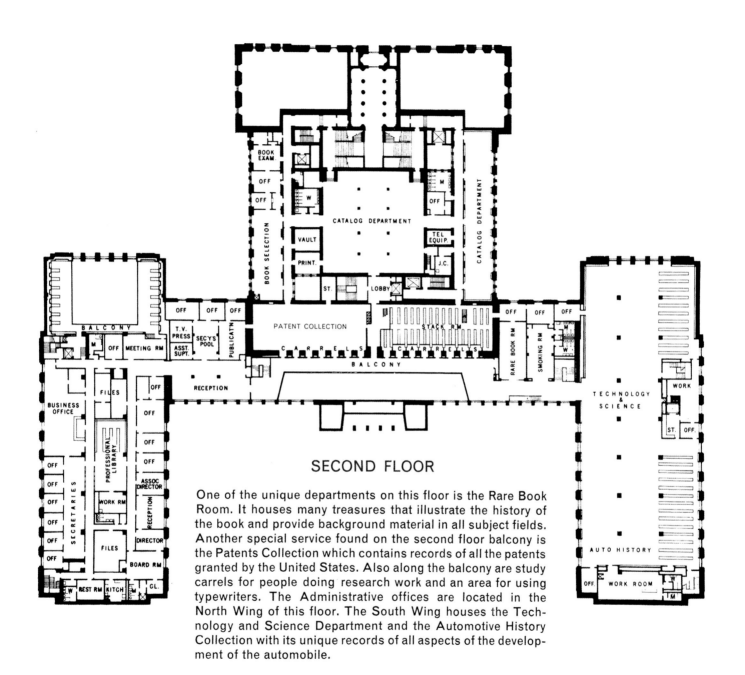

SECOND FLOOR

One of the unique departments on this floor is the Rare Book Room. It houses many treasures that illustrate the history of the book and provide background material in all subject fields. Another special service found on the second floor balcony is the Patents Collection which contains records of all the patents granted by the United States. Also along the balcony are study carrels for people doing research work and an area for using typewriters. The Administrative offices are located in the North Wing of this floor. The South Wing houses the Technology and Science Department and the Automotive History Collection with its unique records of all aspects of the development of the automobile.

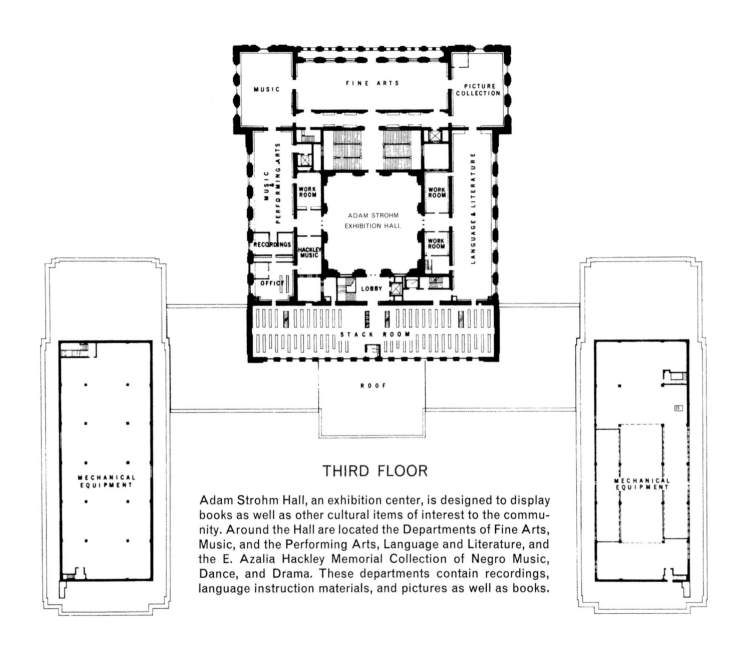

THIRD FLOOR

Adam Strohm Hall, an exhibition center, is designed to display books as well as other cultural items of interest to the community. Around the Hall are located the Departments of Fine Arts, Music, and the Performing Arts, Language and Literature, and the E. Azalia Hackley Memorial Collection of Negro Music, Dance, and Drama. These departments contain recordings, language instruction materials, and pictures as well as books.

THE TWENTY-FIRST-CENTURY LIBRARY

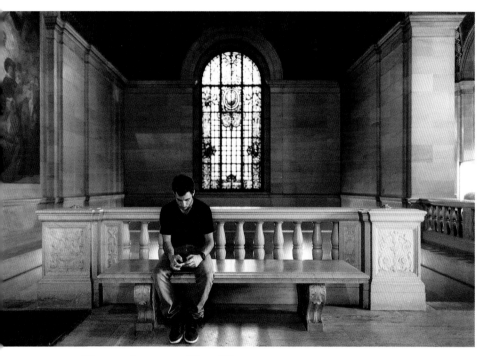

Photograph courtesy of Sam Sklar.

Today's libraries still lend books. But they also provide other services to communities, such as free access to computers and Wi-Fi, story times to children, language classes to immigrants and technology training to everyone. Public libraries are arguably more important today than ever before. Their mission is still the same— to provide free access to information to all people. The way people access information has changed, but they still need the information to succeed, and libraries are providing that.

TONY MARX, PRESIDENT, NEW YORK PUBLIC LIBRARY, NATIONAL PUBLIC RADIO HISTORY DEPARTMENT, MAY 5, 2015

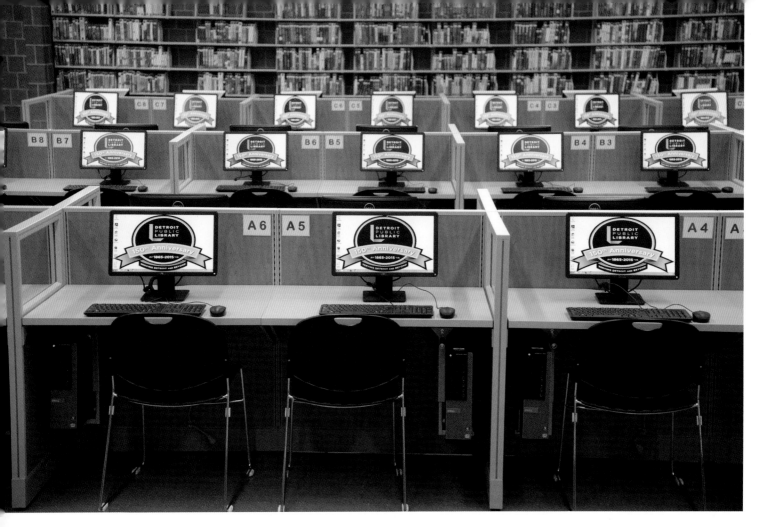

Today the library serves as a technology, learning, and resource center for its citizens and visitors. *Photograph courtesy of Kenneth Gabriel.*

FACING PAGE: The former Children's Library now serves as the HYPE (Helping Young People Excel) Teen Center. *Photograph © Jeffrey A. Scherer, FAIA.*

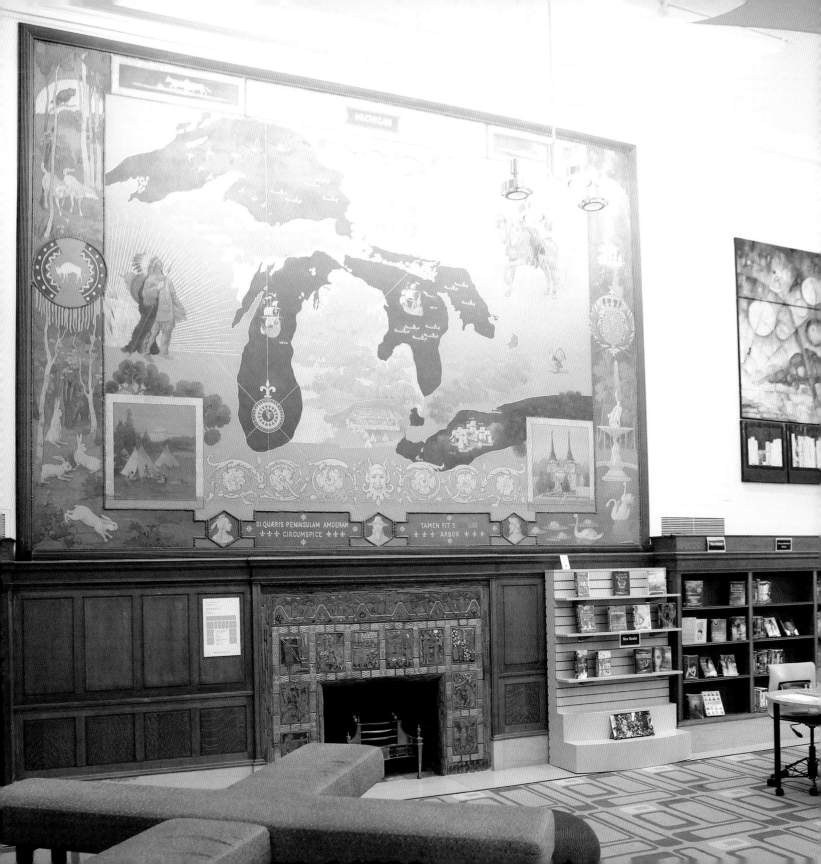

SI QVÆRIS PENINSVLAM AMOENAM
✦ ✦ ✦ CIRCVMSPICE ✦ ✦ ✦

TAMEN FIT S...VS
ARBOR

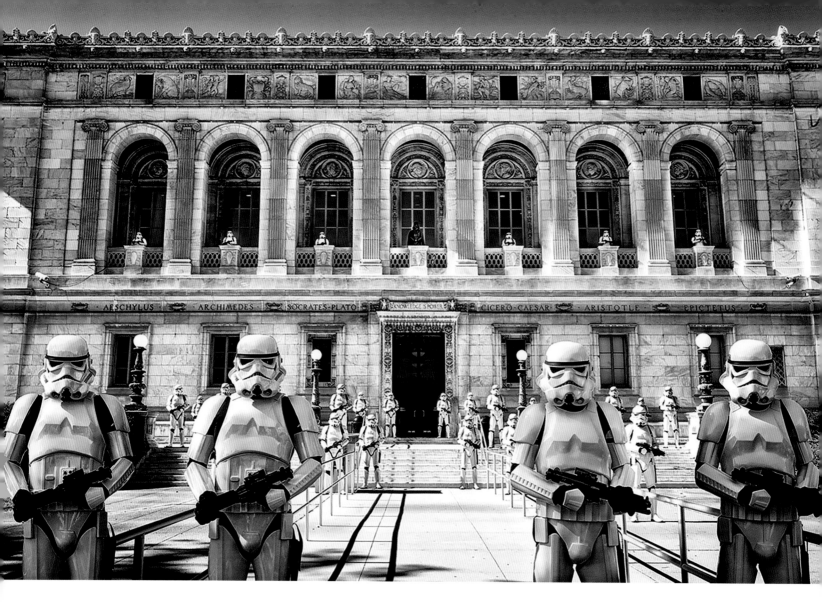

The Main Library facade overcome by The Force. Darth Vader stands in the center arch of the loggia overlooking Stormtroopers on the library steps and promenade. *Photograph courtesy of Shawn Scott.*

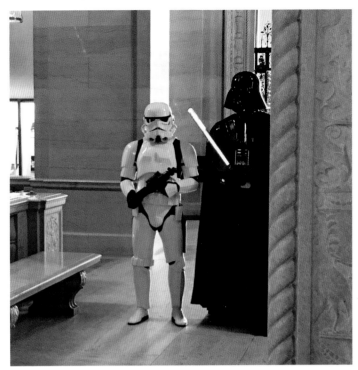

TOP: The Detroit Public Library offers a wide array of enrichment activities meant to entertain and welcome visitors. Darth Vader and a Stormtrooper stand at the ready at the top of the Grand Staircase. *Photograph courtesy of Sean Ryan Everett.*

BOTTOM: Future Leader Dog engages in a library tour as a training exercise. *Photograph courtesy of Barbary Madgy Cohn.*

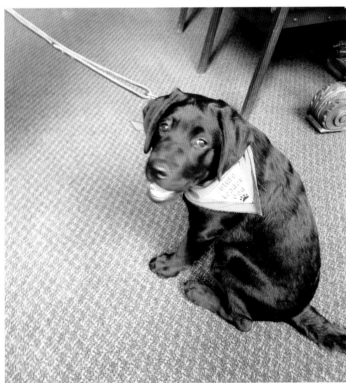

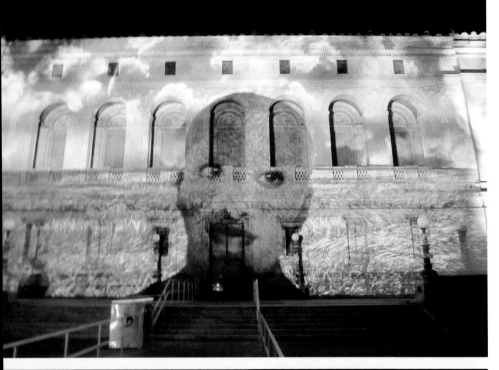

The Woodward Avenue exterior provides a stunning backdrop for DLECTRICITY, September 2014. Inspired by Nuit Blanche arts festivals from around the world, DLECTRICITY provides a sea of light originating through installations of video projection, 3D video mapping, lasers, interactive design, and engineering. *Photographs courtesy of Kenneth Gabriel.*

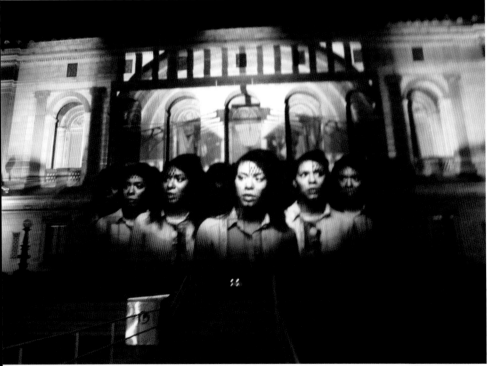

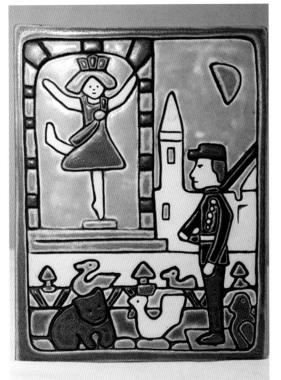

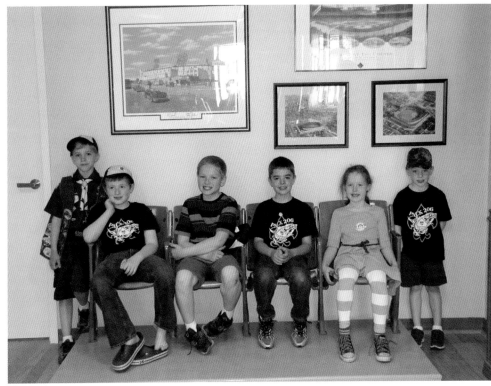

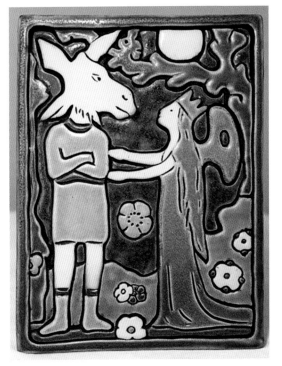

ABOVE, RIGHT: In 1966, Detroit Tigers broadcasting legend Ernie Harwell made an initial donation of his collection of sports materials to the Detroit Public Library. In 2004, the Lulu and Ernie Harwell Room was opened, inviting visitors young and old to experience the history of baseball. *Photograph courtesy of Melissa Gerber.*

LEFT: The Detroit Public Library Friends Foundation, in partnership with Pewabic Pottery, has produced a limited edition of the original tiles surrounding the fireplace in the Children's Library. To the left *(top)* are the Tin Soldier and *(bottom)* Titania and Bottom from *A Midsummer Night's Dream*, two of the tiles glazed, hand-painted, and fired at Pewabic Pottery, Detroit. *Photographs courtesy of Kenneth Gabriel.*

In December 2013, the Detroit Public Library Friends Foundation created a new tour program. *Discover the Wonders of the Detroit Public Library: An Art and Architectural Tour* invites people of all ages to experience an architectural achievement of elegance and grandeur. *Photographs courtesy of Kenneth Gabriel.*

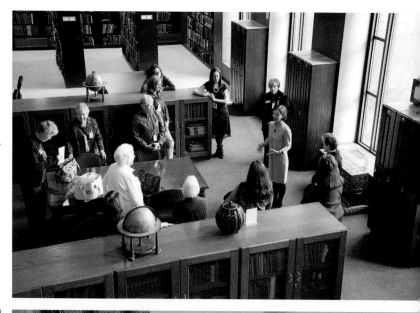

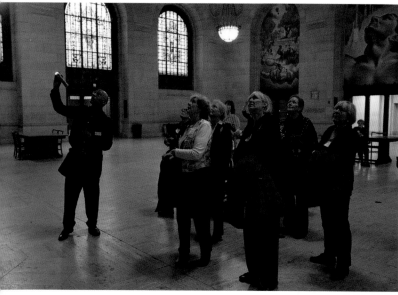

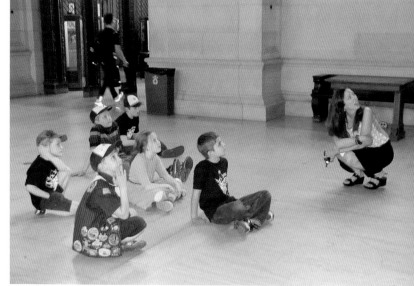

GAIL ROSENBLOOM KAPLAN (1954–)

Gail Rosenbloom Kaplan is a Michigan native. She received her bachelor of fine arts degree from the University of Michigan in 1976. Her work portfolio includes trompe l'oeil, glass mosaic, print making, and mixed media. Kaplan has gained recognition nationally and was selected for the Gifts of Art exhibition at the Taubman Gallery at the University of Michigan Hospital. Her work has also been displayed internationally through the United States Arts and Embassy Program. Kaplan believes that art has the power to heal, and she demonstrates her philosophy with work in libraries, hospitals, community centers, and senior citizen communities.

DANI KATSIR (1946–)

Born in Hungary in 1946, Dani Katsir immigrated to Israel as a child and grew up on a kibbutz. He served in the Israeli Air Force and upon leaving military service needed to find an occupation that would require working with his hands. In 1983, on a visit to Chicago, Katsir visited a Victorian home, took one look at the beautiful stained glass windows, and discovered his future craft. Katsir began to teach himself to work in stained and fused glass. In 1986, he moved to Michigan and became a full-time glass artist. Katsir specializes in three-dimensional fused glass objects. Ten years ago he began a partnership with Gail Rosenbloom Kaplan to create glass mosaic murals. Together Katsir and Kaplan involve children in the process, having them cut and glue tiny colored glass tiles onto boards that are then incorporated into the finished mural.

MOSAICS:

Read, 2015   *Sports*, 2016
Healthy Living, 2016   *Transportation*, 2016
Under the Sea, 2016   *Earth*, 2017
Music, 2016

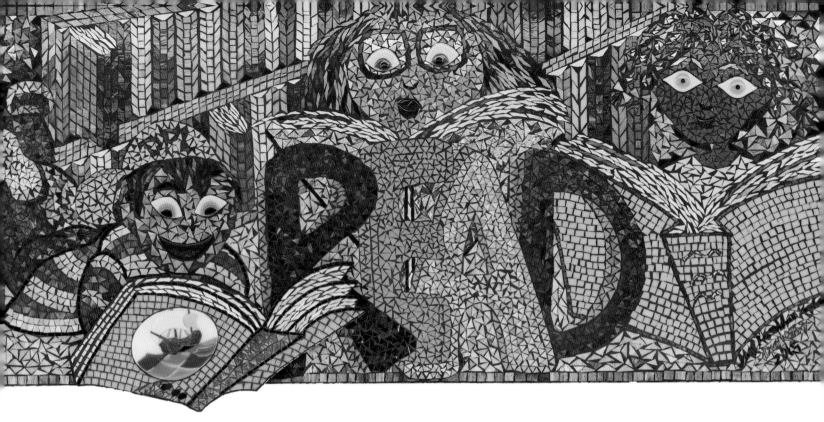

A glass mosaic titled *READ* by Gail Rosenbloom Kaplan and Dani Katsir depicts children engaged in reading. Presented to the Detroit Public Library in honor of Patrice R. Merritt, Executive Director, 2001–2013, from the Detroit Public Library Friends Foundation, June 2015. *Photographs courtesy of Martin Vecchio.*

FACING PAGE: While some may question the need for the public library, the Detroit Public Library continues to inspire the citizens of the twenty-first century. Collections, be they print, electronic, or audio, are utilized by children for schoolwork and fun, and to satisfy their developing intellectual curiosity. *Photographs courtesy of Kenneth Gabriel.*

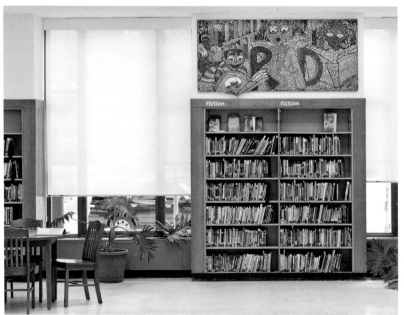

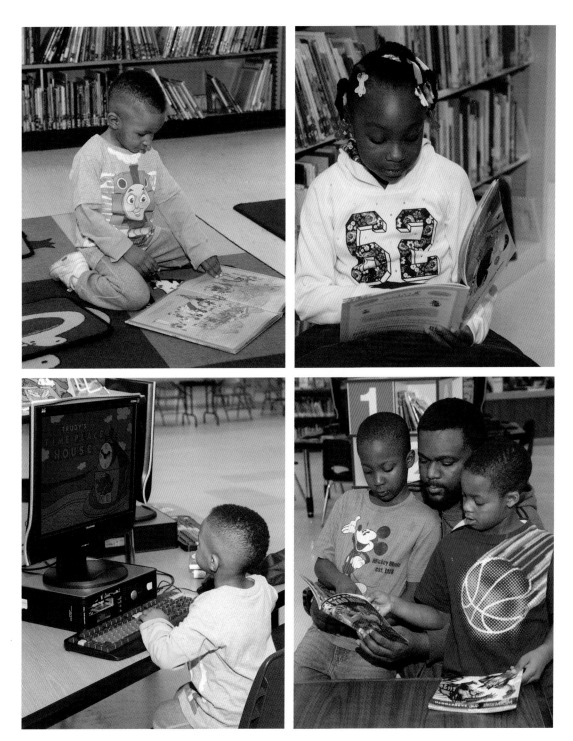

THE TWENTY-FIRST-CENTURY LIBRARY   173

Timothy Ufuomaefe Orikri (1965–)

Timothy Ufuomaefe Orikri was born in 1965 in Delta State, Nigeria, the son of a Baptist minister. He attended Delta State University, graduating in 1991. He studied both Euro-American art and Nigerian art, leading him to discover his own style, which blends both traditions. Orikri moved to the United States in 1995, and his work has been featured in Missouri, Alabama, and throughout Michigan. He currently resides in Detroit.

WORKS, 2008:

Textbooks for Life
The Mind Without Books
Knowledge Is Power
Tale of Two Cities
Tale of Two Cities, II

Inspired by Detroit
Composition ix
The Detroit Library Rendition

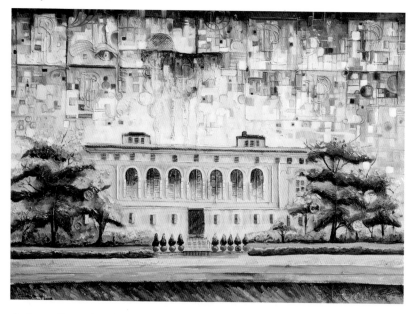

A three-dimensional painting of the Main Library hangs near the Burton Reading Room. Dried fruit, clothespins, matchsticks, and feathers are incorporated into this unique rendition. *Photograph courtesy of John Campbell.*

ACKNOWLEDGMENTS

This book was designed to be a community collaboration. We invited Detroit-area photographers, photography clubs, and classes to come to the Main Library and share with us their artistic vision of the building as captured through photography. The response to our request was overwhelming. Many talented individuals were generous in spirit by offering their work for consideration to this project. We remain most grateful to Amanda "Mac" MacDermaid of Buchanan House Photography; John Campbell; Trista Dymond; Pat Eisenberger of Hall of Learning; Paul Erickson; Kenneth Gabriel; Melissa Gerber; Timothy Griffin, William N. Lawrence Jr.; Jeffrey S. Scherer, FAIA; Shawn Scott; Sam Sklar; Joy VanBuhler; Martin Vecchio; and William Zbaren, for allowing us to use their images in providing a visual tour of the Detroit Public Library.

Our volunteer docents serve as the ambassadors for the *Discover the Wonders of the Detroit Public Library: An Art and Architectural Tour*. We are so grateful for their willingness to share their time and for their desire to become volunteers in support of this important initiative. These individuals joined the tour program without any expectation as to its success or sustainability. They came out of love for the Detroit Public Library and the desire to share its treasures with the public. Without their fortitude and hard work, the tour and now this volume would never have come to pass. We offer a special thanks to Marilyn Battiste, Tudi Harwood, Sue Kalisky, Anne Klisman, Carol Marti, Laura Matheny, Josephine Mondrala, Mary Paquette-Abt, Marilyn

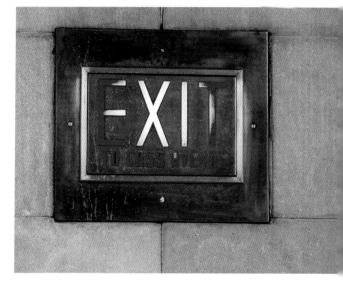

Photograph courtesy of Joy VanBuhler.

Smith, Jane Strand, Chuck Thompson, Iris Lee Underwood, Michael Wells, Karlyta Williams, and Dave Zaleski.

James Evenhuis, volunteer extraordinaire of the Burton Historical Collection at the Detroit Public Library became our official historiographer, a title reserved for only the finest of researchers. His guidance in providing insight as to the "who, what, when, and where" of the Main Library was another inspiration for the *Discover the Wonders* tour. He remains a staunch supporter of our efforts and we remain indebted to him for sharing his vast knowledge about the library.

At every step, we were assisted by the staff of the library's Digital Lab. With their guidance, we were able to appreciate the history of this magnificent edifice visually through its historical records. Our deepest appreciation to Carla Reczek, librarian of the Digital Lab, who always offered "just one more photo" and "one more interesting fact" as she adopted this project as her personal treasure hunt. And to Enid Clark and Vickie Pride, Digital Services assistants, thank you for always being willing to scan yet another image for inclusion in this volume.

The assistance of the staff of the Special Collections of the library was invaluable. Our deep gratitude goes to Mark Bowden, Coordinator of Special Collections at the Detroit Public Library, and to Dawn Eurich, Romie Minor, and Joyce Middlebrooks of the Burton Historical Collection. We were always seeking a map, a floor plan, an image, or another confirmation of a fact. They were always ready to answer our endless questions about image availability.

The Detroit Public Library Security Team accommodated our numerous requests for the tour schedule and photographer access to the building during non-operating hours. The security team also assisted as ambassadors, greeting tour guests and visitors, answering questions, and making all feel welcome. Their support and encouragement in promoting the tour program from inception are two of the reasons this book has come to fruition. We would like to express our gratitude to Talisha Williams, security manager, and Derick Suppon, assistant security manager, as well as to security officers Bradley

Blanks, Ronald Bryant, Shauwn Calvin, Kenneth Cannon, Lawrence Dorsey II, Alexis Griffin, William Martin, Robert Miller, Shim Shun Muqaribu, Carla Myles, Jameka Robison, Edward Scholl, and Michael Turner.

We thank Randy Gies, director of facilities at the Detroit Public Library, for assisting with access to the facility and making improvements to better accommodate our touring guests. His willingness to provide the use of a mechanical lift for photographer use was vital. Some of the images contained within the volume could not have been captured without his assistance. Also, David Kaszubowski and Keith Brooks of the Main Library's ground maintenance crew were always willing to trim a few bushes in our pursuit to better view exterior details and to move interior plantings for better viewing of architectural detail during tours. Special thanks to Randall Williams Design for design of the tour's architectural labels.

The Detroit Public Library Friends Foundation and its board of directors supported the implementation of the tour program. Proceeds from the sale of this book will be given to the foundation in support of their efforts on behalf of the Detroit Public Library. We would like to personally thank Sean Ryan Everett, director of the foundation, for serving as a tour docent and photographer, and as always a cheerleader of this undertaking. We also thank the Friends Foundation for its financial support of this volume and making it most worthy of the great institution that the foundation supports through its fundraising efforts.

We would like to extend very special gratitude to the Honorable Avern Cohn for his support of this publication and his advocacy of the *Discover the Wonders* tour. It was Judge Cohn who prompted Barbara to contact the Friends Foundation and garner support for the creation of the tour. To both the judge and his wife, Lois, we extend our appreciation for their ongoing encouragement.

And finally to our families, who endured months of talk about tours and photos, and who allowed us to overtake the family dining room table, a guest room floor, or other home area to display photo after photo for consideration and inclusion in this volume. To Sheldon Cohn and our children, Jonathan and Jeremy, thank you for your support and patience and for inspiring me (Barbara) to express myself in ways I never thought imaginable. To my (Patrice's) husband, Grady Merritt, who was vigilant in inquiring about the book's progress and listened time and again to the uncertainty as to whether it would ever come to print, thank you for your love and encouragement. His comments about an impending "book party" forever kept my hopes alive. Parents are often named as heroes, and ours are no exception. We remain forever inspired by their high regard of our accomplishments and support even in times of failure. Without their inspiration for the rich rewards of hard work and the spirit of volunteerism we would never have taken on such a daunting project. Thank you, Max and Phyllis Madgy and Samuel and Antoinette Rafail.

The Wayne State University Press staff were enthusiastic believers in this project from day one. Kathryn Peterson Wildfong, associate director and editor-in-chief, held our hands throughout the publishing process, reminding us always that we had done "a fine job" as the most organized of author novices. Her patience and expert guidance made us believe in ourselves. To Trudi Gershinov, of TG Design, thank you for a magnificent book jacket. Ceylan Akturk, rights and permissions editor, kept us honest and accurate. Carrie Downes Teefey, senior production editor, kept the process moving forward and ensuring all deadlines were met. Emily Katherine Nowak, marketing and sales director, showed unbridled enthusiasm in promoting this untold Detroit story, and Jenn Backer, copy editor, offered critical advice and ideas throughout the editing process. Her command of verb tenses was stellar!

And finally, to Andrew Carnegie whose vision and benevolence provided the world with infinite access to knowledge through such wonderful edifices as the Detroit Public Library.

The Detroit Public Library Friends Foundation

After its establishment in 1865, the Detroit Public Library fared well in accumulating large numbers of books and documents as well as rare and unusual items that served the needs of researchers and scholars. Although materials were gratefully received, cash donations were infrequent, making it difficult to purchase items that would add to the library's reputation as a repository of choice.

On the evening of September 24, 1942, a group of thirty-eight Detroit-area citizens met in the Main Library and organized the Friends of the Detroit Public Library, Inc. Those who were present had been invited to attend by an unofficial committee who, through a series of discussions, called an organizational meeting. The people invited shared one common denominator: an interest in books and a desire to help the Detroit Public Library. Library director Ralph A. Ulveling explained the purpose of the organization: to encourage public interest in and contributions to the library's collection of rare books, manuscripts, and other important material and to provide funds from membership, gifts, and bequests for the purpose of benefiting the library. Another implied purpose was to create a strong public relations campaign that would engage the public in library activities.

The nation was at war, but bylaws were adopted, a slate of officers was presented, and articles of incorporation were prepared and submitted. The Friends of the Detroit Public Library was incorporated by the State of Michigan on October 12, 1942, making it one of the oldest—if not the oldest—Friends organizations in the country.

In June 2004, the Executive Committee, in working with the Detroit Public Library administration, determined that library needs were to become more capital in nature. While the Friends would continue to support the library's historically successful programs and library collections, it needed to seek larger and more substantial gifts. The past was very much a part of the organizational future and a new name, the Detroit Public Library Friends Foundation, was ratified by the membership.

PHOTOGRAPHERS

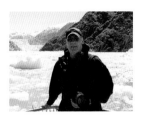

JOHN CAMPBELL has been a photographer for more than forty years. He teaches photography at Schoolcraft College in Livonia, gives presentations on photography, and conducts photo workshops. His tagline is "I carry my camera with humor, compassion and curiosity."

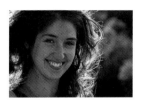

TRISTA DYMOND is a twelve-year, Detroit-based photographer, graphic designer, and visual artist who first studied fine art at Pratt at Munson Williams Proctor Arts Institute and received her bachelor's degree in fine arts from the College for Creative Studies in 2009 in interior design. She has since worked with Tyree Guyton at the Heidelberg Project and started her own creative small business under the name Dymond Creative. Trista's drive is to celebrate and promote self-worth (individually and collectively) through the universal language of creativity.

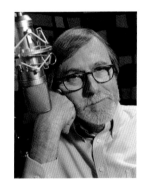

PAUL ERICKSON, of Beverly Hills, Michigan, has been a radio personality, musician, record producer, and photographer, though not all at once. An alumnus of Wayne State University, Paul has a BFA and an MAT, and is trying to find out what the letters mean.

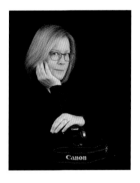

PAT EISENBERGER is an emerging artist who uses the latest techniques in digital photography to enhance her creative vision. Her home state of Michigan inspires her work with its beautiful forests and lakes, and its magnificent cities and architecture.

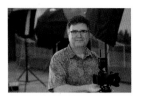

KENNETH A. GABRIEL has reinvented himself from a former roofer to information system network technician. The one thing that has remained constant in his life is his passion for photography. He has an eye for detail and a unique and creative vision that is evident in his images.

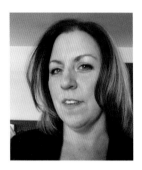

MELISSA GERBER is a preschool teacher who is happiest when spending time with her husband, Brian, and their five children. When she is not volunteering, she enjoys taking photos, reading, and spending time at her cabin in northern Michigan.

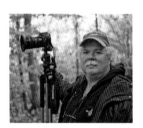

TIMOTHY GRIFFIN's mission as a photographer is to use his skills and abilities to capture his subject in a setting and manner that will show it in a natural state. As an instructor, he has been able to pass on his passion for using both his creativity and knowledge of technology to make great photographs.

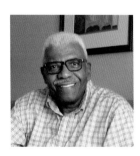

WILLIAM N. LAWRENCE JR. was born and raised in Detroit. He graduated from the University of Detroit with a bachelor of arts degree and earned his master's in social work from Wayne State University. Retired from the Wayne County Circuit Court, he is an avid photographic hobbyist who loves traveling and taking pictures.

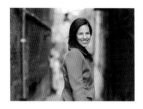

AMANDA "MAC" MACDER-MAID is a metro Detroit real estate agent and photographer. She enjoys capturing Detroit's historic beauty.

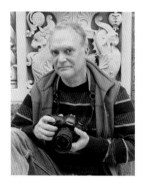

JEFF MORRISON is an award-winning photographer who has been taking pictures since his parents gave him his first camera at age nine. He has a bachelor's degree in history from Eastern Michigan University and lives in Oxford, Michigan, with his wife, Susie, and their dog, Manfred. He is currently working on *Guardians of Detroit: A Pictorial Guide to Architectural Sculpture in the Motor City. Photo by suecsuecsue.*

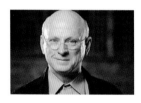

JEFFREY S. SCHERER is a founding principal of MSR, with 44 years of design expertise in libraries and commercial office buildings, including more than 125 libraries across the United States. Known for leading the discussion and writing on important issues surrounding libraries today, he is a frequent conference lecturer on the role of the library in society. Scherer was elected into the American Institute of Architects College of Fellows in 1998.

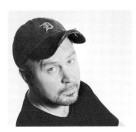

SHAWN M. SCOTT is a metro Detroit photographer who captures everything from weddings to architecture. His true passion, however, is creating sci-fi urban photography.

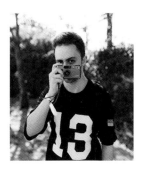

SAM SKLAR is a twenty-one-year-old photographer from Metro Detroit. He is expected to graduate from business school in 2017 and spends most of his time traveling and documenting his experiences under the moniker *sklvr*.

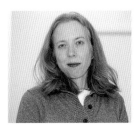

JOY VANBUHLER is a native Detroit photographer. Her five-year and counting picture-a-day project has amassed a large array of diverse images of life in Michigan. From the Detroit architecture to stunning landscapes, from wildlife to everyday life, these pictures capture the beauty of Michigan. Since she began photographing, her images have been featured in books, environmental reports, and newsletters.

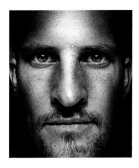

MARTIN VECCHIO graduated with honors from Wayne State University in 2008 with a bachelor's degree in fine arts with concentrations in photography and graphic design. He honed and developed his skills as a commercial automotive photography assistant and digital technician. Vecchio has been a resident of the city of Detroit since 2003. He finds that it's the jewels of the city both large and small, from the incredible institutions to single incredible individuals, that keep him here, photographing them all.

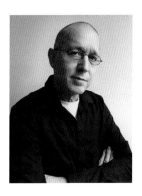

WILLAM ZBAREN'S books include the award-winning *American City: Detroit Architecture, 1845–2005* and *American City: St. Louis Architecture: Three Centuries of Classic Design*. He also shoots regularly for the *New York Times* and other publications.